A Murder Most Unsolved

Copyright © 2025 by Sarah Dosher

All rights reserved. No part of this publication may be reproduced, stored in any retrieval system, or transmitted, in any form or by any means, electronic, mechanical, photocopying, recording or otherwise, without the prior written permission in writing.

This book is a work of fiction. Names, characters, business, organizations, places and events other than those clearly in the public domain, are either the product of the author's imagination or are used fictitiously. Any resemblance to actual persons, living or dead, events or locales is entirely coincidental.

For my family, friends, and beloved readers who stuck around during my decade long publishing nap. You have the patience of saints, and possibly questionable taste in writers, but I'm forever grateful you're still here.

1

THE BOOKSTORE HEIR APPARENT

Then

The bookstore smelled like old paper, cinnamon scones, and the dust motes that floated in the sunbeams.

Ten-year-old Freddie March sat cross-legged behind the counter at The Marple & Quill with her nose buried in a copy of *The Secret of the Old Clock*. Her feet kicked idly beneath her, heels tapping the worn wooden floor while her eyes devoured the words on the page. Somewhere outside, a bicycle bell trilled past the window and, farther away, the church bell gave a lazy half-hour clonk as if it could barely be bothered to alert the citizens of the ever-changing time. Fernridge always sounded like this: human and small yet busy with ordinary things.

"I hope you know," her grandmother Winnie said, sliding a tray of chocolate chip scones into the display case, "that book you're reading is banned in six imaginary kingdoms for being too clever, and the sequel is banned in even more."

Freddie grinned. "Then I definitely want to read the next book too!"

Winnie chuckled and perched herself on the stool beside her granddaughter, mindlessly brushing crumbs off her apron. Winnie always wore aprons in the shop, even though she hadn't baked in years. Technically, the closest she got was handling the baked goods while she transferred them from the delivery trays into the display case. Freddie suspected the apron made her feel more like a character in one of the quaint stories she loved. In Fernridge, people tried on new personalities the way other towns tried on fancy clothes for a special occasion. Here, it wasn't the fancier the better, though it was the more unusual the better.

"You know, darling," Winnie said, her voice dropping lower now, more serious, "books are the best kind of magic. When you open one, your world shifts. Time slows. You breathe in someone else's thoughts, part of them."

Freddie tilted her head. "Better than spells?"

"Much better." Winnie tapped her finger on the cover of Freddie's book. "Spells wear off. Stories we've read never leave us; they become part of us."

"I think I want to live in a cool bookstore when I grow up, just like you," Freddie finally said after taking time to consider her grandmother's thoughts on books.

Winnie smiled, soft and wistful. "Well then, it's lucky I've got just such a bookstore you can have one day. And it's even luckier for me, because I only trust one person in the entire world to watch over it for me."

Freddie's eyes lit up. "Really?"

"Yes, really. It won't actually be much different, just transferring from the first Winifred March to the second Winifred March. Winnie and Freddie," she said while tapping Freddie playfully on the nose.

Outside, the wind rustled the chimes above the door, and Aggie the cat, in all his regal plumpness, sat upon his chosen throne atop the bookstore's coveted mystery section, batting at a small paperback in an attempt to knock it to the ground. Satisfaction spread wide across his little orange face once his mission was finally accomplished.

"You better not damage the merchandise, Agatha Purr-ristie!" Winnie scoffed at the mischievous cat. Freddie knew the cat was in big trouble because Winnie rarely used Aggie's full name, the cat version of her favorite author, Agatha Christie.

A warm draft carried in the scents of cut grass and honeysuckle from the town square through the open door. Freddie breathed deeper, trying to remember this perfect day and perfect place forever.

Winnie reached behind the counter, pulling out a paper crown she had made earlier with way too much glitter. She placed it gently on Freddie's head. "I hereby name you Bookstore Heir Apparent. Long may you read."

Freddie giggled and sat up straighter, proud and royal. A bookstore heir suited her just fine. She liked reading and puzzles; she liked figuring out how things fit, which is why mystery books were her favorite, just like Winnie. At school, she raced through books while other kids dawdled. Here, it felt like she could solve the whole world if she just read enough. Winnie always told her, "Books contain all the mysteries of the universe, which means they contain all the solutions as well."

Swift footsteps interrupted the moment as Freddie's mother, Susan, appeared in the entryway, clutching her purse across her chest like a shield. Her face was pinched and pale, and her words came harsh and quick. "Freddie. We need to go, now!"

"So soon?" Winnie asked, brows knitting in clear concern. She wiped her hands on her apron and stepped toward her. "Come inside, dear, you look pale. Sit a minute. The kettle's still hot."

"I don't have time for tea," Susan said, her voice cracked, betraying her mood and exhaustion.

"We always have time for tea." Winnie crossed to the counter, poured a cup, and pressed it gently into her daughter-in-law's hands. "Two sugars, just how you like it."

Susan hesitated before taking a sip. A small flicker of relief passed over her face, softening her tight jaw. For a fleeting instant, she looked younger, less burdened.

"You're too kind to me, you always have been," she said, almost accusingly.

Winnie's smile was gentle. "That's what family is for. To be kind when the world isn't." She rested one hand briefly on the younger woman's arm.

"She doesn't know yet," Susan whispered as she turned her back to Freddie, attempting to block her voice. "I found the note this morning. He's gone, Winifred. Just... gone. I don't want her to grow up haunted by this town or by his absence. If he can't be here, neither will we, and we're not coming back, ever."

Winnie's voice was steady, but softer than before. "You can't protect her by cutting her off from everything she knows and loves."

"She doesn't need reminders," Susan snapped, the tea trembled in her cup. "She needs a new start, we both do."

Freddie held her breath. Her father. Gone? She didn't understand. But something settled in her chest, some fear that made her not want to ask questions, not yet.

Winnie turned back with a too-bright smile and knelt beside her. "Your mother says it's time to go, sweetheart."

"But—" Freddie started, pointing to her paper crown.

Winnie touched it gently, adjusting the fold. "This place will wait for you. However long it takes."

And when Susan ushered Freddie toward the door, Winnie added softly, almost to herself, "And I'll wait too."

***

Now

Freddie blinked awake, but the dream was still racing through her mind.

Her apartment was dark, but the room was illuminated by her phone alarm buzzing frantically on the nightstand. She still faintly smelled the lavender she'd sprayed on her pillow the night before, and the hum of her sound machine still rang through the room. On the single, overfilled bookshelf, thrift store paperbacks leaned at brave angles where she'd crammed them to fit. The space had all the personality of a file box, which seemed appropriate for a woman who spent her days in a library archive.

After flipping on her lamp, she rubbed her eyes then stared at the crumpled letter on her comforter, the one she'd read a dozen times but still didn't fully understand. Winnie's handwriting, sharp and slanted, danced across the page.

SARAH DOSHER

You must come back to Fernridge. It's a matter of life and death. Don't tell anyone. Just come back home. Please, Freddie.

Freddie closed her eyes. She hadn't been back since that day. Since she was ten years old and everything safe unraveled. And Winnie had never pressured her to come back, never even told her to come. She'd invited her to different events, birthdays and other celebrations, but she'd never demanded her presence.

She wasn't sure she wanted to go back now. It had been far too long. Her absence had gone on for too many long years.

But Winnie had never been dramatic. Pleasant, always. Theatrical, maybe occasionally. But nothing like this.

She checked the time on her phone. It was so early that even the morning birds weren't up singing yet, but her flight would be leaving before long.

With a groan, Freddie pushed back the covers, dragging herself upright.

Fernridge was calling.

And this time, she wasn't sure it would let her go so easily.

2

WHERE STORIES GROW WILD

Though Freddie survived the early morning flight, just getting into the rental car made her stomach knot. Her damp palms clung to the wheel, as if letting go for even a second might send her spinning off course.

Why was she so nervous to see her grandmother again?

She eyed the winding country road with the kind of caution usually reserved for bomb disposal or cleaning Bengal tiger teeth.

"Okay," she embarrassingly muttered to herself. "You're a grown, almost thirty-year-old woman who pays your taxes. You can drive through a town with one stoplight." She huffed to herself.

The GPS chirped, relentlessly cheerful and unstressed, "In two miles, your destination will be on the right."

"Thanks, traitor," Freddie muttered, half to the GPS, half to the still-growing knot in her stomach.

She adjusted her glasses, peered through the windshield, and took a long, steadying drink from the Diet Coke she'd grabbed at the airport. The first bubbles burned her throat in exactly the way she craved. She'd need an endless supply of Diet Coke to survive this day.

The air here was different than it was in the city. It was softer, somehow. Velvety, but also a little damp, carrying the faint smell of earth and honeysuckle. In the city, her days were measured by the hum of fluorescent bulbs and the click of climate-control vents. Here, the world seemed to slowly exhale.

She leaned into the next curve—and slammed on the brakes.

A goat—no, two—trotted across the road, head held high in indignation, as if *she* had been the one in the wrong. One of them gave a loud "*Baaaaaa*" and actually headbutted her bumper before continuing its self-important strut to the other side.

A man on a bicycle appeared seconds later, pedaling slowly and waving at her as he passed, a fishing pole bouncing from the basket attached to his handlebars.

"Morning!" he called cheerfully, as if near livestock collisions were just a regular daily thing.

Freddie blinked. "Of course. Why wouldn't there be angry goats and a fisherman on a bicycle?"

Still rattled, she eased forward, shoulders tight with tension and eyes peeled for any more rogue livestock. The road curved again, sloping between green hills, and then suddenly, there it was.

Fernridge.

Just like she remembered. Well, it seemed smaller. And somehow brighter.

The welcome sign stood at the edge of town, chipped at the corners but freshly painted with cheerful lettering:

Welcome to Fernridge
Est. 1901
Where stories grow wild

Someone had taped a large handmade poster beneath it for the Annual Pie & Poetry Picnic, featuring what looked like a goose wearing a bike helmet while riding a scooter. The goose's wings flapped wildly while its eyes were wide and manic. Freddie laughed and shook her head at the cuteness.

Beyond the sign was a rusting water tower standing guard, with a faded **GO FERNRIDGE GEESE!** still plastered on the side from some forgotten sports season. A convenience store marquee promised **HOT DOGS & SOD**. She sincerely hoped there was a missing "A" on the last word. Either way, she knew she'd be back for another Diet Coke before the end of the day.

Freddie felt the first tug of a smile, half nerves, half nostalgia, as she grew closer to The Marple & Quill.

As she crossed into town, the houses shifted from bland vinyl siding to charmingly crooked front porch cottages. An array of potted flowers stood in rows with porch swings creaking lazily in the light breeze. Each house had a wind chime tinkling in mismatched harmonies. American flags fluttered on doorways alongside sunflower wreaths. There were hand-painted yard signs advertising peach jam, goat yoga, and, one foreboding sign nailed crooked to a fence post that read, **LOST CHICKEN. DO NOT APPROACH**.

The next block, she saw a kid in shorts and cowboy boots walking a dachshund in a cable-knit sweater next to two older men who argued good-naturedly under a barber pole, one of them gesturing with his tobacco pipe for emphasis. Freddie passed it all slowly, drinking it in, each small moment like a brushstroke on a canvas she hadn't seen in years.

And then, like a long-lost memory unfolding, The Marple & Quill came into view.

Freddie's chest tightened.

It was nestled on the corner of Main Street and Elder Lane, flanked by a sleepy office building on one side and a bakery that smelled like heaven on the other. The shop's green awning had faded to sea-glass over the years, but the little brass bell above the door gleamed in the sun as though it had been polished every morning since she'd been gone.

Her throat went tight as tears burned her eyes.

But as she sat there admiring this place she once loved so much, she could feel something was off.

No early birds were milling around the front steps with coffee cups in hand, trading gossip before work. No warm light spilling from the windows. No chalkboard out front boasting that Today's Special was Murderously Good Scones.

The **CLOSED** sign still hung on the front door.

The bookstore looked still, like someone had pressed the pause button on it.

Freddie felt her eyes squint in confusion. Winnie should have been up long before dawn, bustling in the shop, fussing with the bakery display, and making her coffee and tea that was too strong, but somehow just right.

She got out of her car and stepped closer, heart pounding.

The front door was ajar. Just slightly, but enough for a sliver of shadow to escape into the sunlight.

Her stomach dropped.

She pushed it open gently as the brass bell above the door gave its practiced chime. Only this time it echoed strangely, too loud amongst the quiet.

Inside, the shop was dim. The curtains were still drawn, and the soft glow of reading lamps was missing. Dust floated in the air, and the faint scent of cinnamon and lemon polish had grown stale.

There was something unnatural in the silence. Like a stage set moments before curtain—books frozen mid-shuffle, a receipt half-spooled in the register, a pen without a cap beside an unfinished to-do list.

She saw that books were scattered across the floor, and one of the display tables was tilted with a broken leg, and what looked like a teacup display was shattered beneath it in a mess of porcelain shards.

"Winnie?" Freddie called softly, her voice shaking.

No answer came.

Her heartbeat climbed, quick and hard, as she stepped further in. Her shoes crunched faintly on the broken porcelain. The silence pressed in on her ears, so thick it made her head ache.

And then she saw her.

In the far corner of the shop, nestled in the old floral wingback chair by the fireplace. It was the same chair she always claimed during lazy afternoons. There sat Winnie.

Her eyes were closed, and she had a teacup resting delicately in her hand, and a book lay open in her lap.

Relief surged through Freddie. Winnie had fallen asleep waiting for her. Of course. That had to be it.

"Winnie," she whispered, smiling weakly. "You scared me. Why's the shop such a mess? Are you—"

Her words faltered. Something was wrong.

Her grandmother was too still, and Freddie swore her chest didn't rise. The teacup was half-full, but as Freddie reached out and brushed her fingers along its side, the porcelain was cold. She saw that her lips were pale and her skin ashen.

The book was frozen mid-chapter as if it had been waiting for a hand that would never turn another page.

Freddie's vision narrowed, and a roaring sound filled her ears, as though the world had tilted, and everything went rushing down a drain.

"No..." she whispered.

She reached for her, her hand hovered, trembling, inches from Winnie's sleeve. She wanted to shake her, wake her, and undo this. She wanted to run out the door and pretend she had never stepped inside.

But she already knew.

Winifred March, her grandmother, her constant, her anchor in a world that too often felt adrift, was dead.

And that meant everything was very, very wrong.

3

Murder Muffins

The tea was too sweet, the blanket too warm, and the sunlight too cheerful.

Freddie sat stiffly in one of the bookshop's worn reading chairs with her legs curled up beneath her and her hands wrapped around a chipped mug of chamomile tea that someone had pressed into them like a prescription. The blanket around her shoulders smelled like dust and old upholstery.

It had been about an hour since she found Winnie. An hour since her world split into before and after.

Outside, the sun dared to shine like nothing had happened. The glass storefront sparkled, and a breeze lifted the edges of the flyers on the corkboard by the door, Founders Day Bake-Off, Historical Society "Show & Tell" (Bring Your Strangest Teapot). The flowers in the window box bobbed gently, waving a greeting to all who passed by.

Freddie stared through it all, numb. She thought of her tiny apartment with its flickering bulb and the comforting hum of the building's old radiator, and felt a tug of homesickness for a life that she knew was grayscale. Here, everything was oversaturated: the colors, the smells, the memories. Her life in the city was small, but so far, things in Fernridge were so painful that she longed for the bleakness of the city and her apartment.

Across the shop, a uniformed police officer stood near the front desk, flipping through half-blank pages, then stopping to tap her pen on her teeth and stare off into the middle distance before she came up with another tidbit she'd eagerly jot in her awaiting folio. She looked to be in her late twenties, with a precise ponytail and an expression that said she trusted no one and liked even fewer. The badge clipped to her chest read Deputy Barrett.

Every few minutes, the officer would glance over at Freddie—not unkindly, but suspiciously, like she wasn't quite convinced Freddie hadn't killed someone before she'd even had her breakfast.

Freddie looked back down into her tea willing it to improve her current state of mind.

The bell above the door jingled.

"Winnie?" called a bright voice. "You in the back? I've got the cinnamon-sugar Murder Muffins, just like you asked for, though I'm starting to wonder if naming baked goods after crimes is affecting your sales..." Her voice trailed off.

The woman stepped into view, holding a large bakery box and wearing a sunflower-yellow dress, a lopsided apron, and a look of sunny obliviousness. Then she saw the police officer and the crime scene tape.

The box nearly slipped from her fingers. "Holy hell," she breathed.

Freddie blinked at her through bleary eyes.

The woman turned toward her, confusion softening to concern. "Wait a minute... Freddie?"

Recognition bloomed slowly across the woman's face. Her eyes widened. "Oh, sweetheart, what are you doing here? What is going on?" she whispered while frantically looking from side to side, then stepping forward.

That was the moment something cracked, and Freddie dissolved into tears.

The woman, Pru Hawthorn, was Winnie's best friend. Freddie had so many memories of the two women from her childhood. Many of them featured the two getting themselves into mischief, but they almost always came out unscathed with an entertaining story to tell.

Pru was in her later years, though she wouldn't dare say her exact age; she was all soft curves and practical strength from years of kneading dough and hauling trays. She had the kind of presence that filled a room before she even opened her mouth, which was helped along by her riot of chestnut waves, which she rarely managed to keep pinned back under her round face. Her cheeks were often pink from the ovens, her forearms dusted in flour no matter the hour of the day. Her penchant for bold lipsticks made her brown eyes sparkle with kindness, even when her words carried her signature edge of judgment.

Pru set the bakery box down and wrapped her arms around Freddie without hesitation. Her embrace was warm and sweetly scented. Up close, Pru smelled like butter and sugar and a little like cinnamon hand soap. There was a dusting of flour on her cheekbone and cat hair on the hem of her apron, which somehow made Freddie feel safer.

"It's okay, baby girl. You're okay," she murmured, rocking her gently. "What happened? What the ever-lovin'—" Her voice was covered by the heaving sound of Freddie's tears. "I've been up since 3:30 and I am too tired to be delicate, so just sit here and breathe with me."

A few minutes later, Pru sat beside Freddie, one hand resting protectively over her hands as the police officer gave a dry summary of what they knew so far.

"No signs of forced entry, just an unlocked door left ajar. Tea was ice cold when Miss March found her, the book still set open in her lap. We're waiting on the coroner, but preliminarily... it appears to be a heart attack. Peaceful."

Pru frowned. "But Winnie didn't have a heart condition. And what about all this?" She gestured to the broken porcelain and scattered books. "You think she did a polka through the display table before calmly having evening tea and dying of a heart attack?"

"That we know of," the officer replied regarding the potential heart condition. "And this could have happened beforehand, and Miss March was simply taking a break from clearing up when it happened." She sighed—knowing as well as everyone else that her guess of the happenings didn't seem likely. "Or that ornery cat that's usually around could have had something to do with smashing the porcelain. I'm not really sure...yet." She turned her eyes to Freddie again. "You said you hadn't seen her in... how long? And you arrived just this morning? We'll need to confirm that."

Freddie sniffed. "I hadn't seen her since I was ten. And yes, I arrived this morning, you can check with the airline."

The officer scribbled that down, then looked at Pru with squinted eyes and furrowed brow. "You know her?"

Pru snorted. "Do I know her? I practically raised her on lemon bars and gossip right here in this bookstore. Haven't seen her in years, though. She grew up and got smart and left us all behind." She softened it with a squeeze of Freddie's hand. "I didn't say I approved, though."

The officer raised an eyebrow. "Huh. You know, I'd heard Miss March talk about her granddaughter quite often, in fact, though I wasn't entirely sure she was real. Seemed like a figment of her very active imagination."

Freddie gave a soft, humorless laugh. "Sometimes I'm not sure I'm real either."

Out of the corner of her eye, something flickered in the back of the room.

Freddie turned her head just in time to catch the swish of a long orange tail disappearing through a door.

But this wasn't just any door; it was a secret door, the coolest of doors. It looked like a bookshelf with three rows of old encyclopedias and a dusty globe perched on top, but the shelving unit stood ajar just enough to reveal a narrow hallway behind it.

Freddie's eyes narrowed.

She'd spent half her childhood in this shop and had never seen that door open. Winnie's apartment had always been a mystery, hidden away like the ending of a good book. Unless a person knew the exact hidden lever to pull, you'd never see the bookshelf opened into the secret entrance.

Pru and the officer were still talking, their voices muffled under the pulse now pounding in Freddie's ears.

Quietly, she set her teacup down, slipped out from under the blanket, and moved toward the secret door.

The hallway was dark, but sunlight filtered in from a high window at the end. The air back here smelled different from out front, with notes of lavender and old wood. From beyond the window, cicadas hummed the way they always did in Fernridge summers, steady and eternal.

Freddie's footsteps were soft on the floorboards as she followed the sound of little feet padding into the back of the apartment.

"Hello?" she called softly and gently.

A rustle answered her. In the far corner of the sitting room, beneath a towering old cabinet, two round yellow eyes glowed in the shadows.

"Aggie?" Freddie questioned.

The cat stared back.

That couldn't be right. Aggie was old when she was a child. There was no way he was still alive.

She crouched slowly, extending her hand. "Aggie, is that really you?"

The cat shifted, ears twitching. When Freddie reached closer, he backed away slightly, giving her a once-over like a suspicious librarian evaluating a late return.

Then, with great deliberation, he sniffed her hand, then headbutted it eagerly, demanding scratches.

Freddie laughed, wiping her teary eyes.

She caught sight of the small, round tag on the cat's collar and gently turned it over.

"Aggie" the Second.

4

RETIRED? NEVER.

Freddie sat in the middle of The Marple & Quill with her hands in her lap and her mind everywhere else.

The police were gone, and the bookstore was quiet again.

The day had shifted to late afternoon, throwing warm golden patches across the floorboards and casting soft shadows behind the shelves. Dust danced in the light, undisturbed as she sat frozen to her current location. She let her gaze drift from the cash register to the windows, to the half-filled bakery case that probably contained yesterday's pastries, to the overdone display (that looked more like a shrine) to Winnie's favorite murder mystery show, *Father Grey*, then to her chamomile teacup still resting on the counter. The smell of distinct lemon polish clung to the counter—Winnie's favorite brand. Freddie hadn't realized she remembered it until now.

Winnie should've been there, fussing about the misshapen scones or rearranging the mystery section based on mood or moon phase or some other such thing. Instead, there was stillness except for Pru humming quietly as she swept up the broken teacups and collected the books scattered across the floor.

Freddie knew Pru wanted to ask her questions. She could feel it in the way the old woman glanced at her from time to time, as if testing the waters by the expression she wore. How long has it been? Why didn't you come back sooner? How could you stay away from your grandmother for so long? Freddie knew all those questions and a million more were just on the tip of Pru's tongue.

But Pru asked none of those prying questions; instead, she asked a different question, over and over.

"Are you okay, sweetie?"

Freddie nodded the first time.

And the second.

And by the fourth, something snapped.

"I'm fine!" she said, too sharply as she thrust her hands down on her thighs in exasperation. The words rang in the air, sharp as the crack of the broken teacup Pru had just finished sweeping away.

But Pru didn't flinch. She just set the broom aside and wiped her hands on her apron. "Well," she said, her voice soft but firm, "I'm going to head back to the bakery, see if the morning rush did any damage. Lord knows I left Kevin alone with the lumpy biscuit dough and finicky customers for far too long. Last time I did that, Mrs. Halpern accused him of attempted pastry manslaughter."

Freddie said nothing; she still sat entirely numb to everything around her.

"You remember Kevin, right?" Pru asked. "My nephew from my failed marriage, well, he works in the bakery now and is about the only thing that keeps me sane most days. My right-hand man, I guess you could say." Pru chuckled a little, trying to get a response of some kind.

Freddie still didn't speak or react. Pru sighed.

A MURDER MOST UNSOLVED

"I'll be back later this evening. Why don't you take your things up to Winnie's apartment? The police said you're not to leave town for now anyway." Pru hesitated at the door. "Make yourself comfortable, sugar. This place is still yours, if you want it." She added, softer, "She wanted you to have it, you know that."

Then she was gone, and all that was left was silence. Usually, Freddie enjoyed the serenity of a quiet room, but not today, and definitely not in this particular room. The quiet was overwhelming in a room that was more accustomed to being filled with love and laughter.

After a while, Freddie finally gathered her bag and suitcase and made her way to the hidden door at the back, Aggie winding around her legs like a furry shadow. She'd barely gotten to look around the apartment after finding Aggie earlier. The overly suspicious police officer hadn't let her get away for long enough.

The apartment behind the bookstore was exactly as she remembered, and nothing like she remembered. The same faint lavender-and-earthy scent. The same worn floral couch under the lace-draped window. The same ticking grandfather clock in the hall.

But there were new things, too. A colorful glass dish full of wrapped candies she didn't recognize, but looked exactly like what she'd expect a grandmother to have in her home. A stack of mystery magazines with Aggie perched on top, watching her a little too closely. An embroidered pillow on the chair that read: **Retired? Never. Murder waits for no one.** On the wall hung a community theatre poster for *Arsenic and Old Lace*—signed **"To Winifred, our patron saint of cookies. Rupert."**

Everywhere she looked, there were pieces of Winnie. And surprisingly, there were pieces of herself, too.

Her photographs covered the fridge, held up by magnets shaped like teacups and cats and one slightly terrifying Sherlock Holmes bust with googly eyes. There she was, Freddie at twelve, holding a science fair trophy. Freddie in college, standing in front of the library. Freddie, last Christmas, in a fuzzy hat, smiling into the camera she knew Winnie never held. They were all photos that Freddie had sent to Winnie over the years. Her grandmother had kept them all and lovingly displayed her in almost every corner of the apartment. An apartment Freddie had refused to return to for over half of her life.

And there, just beneath her photo, a face she hadn't seen in years.

Her father.

The photo was small. Faded. He looked young. Happy. Alive in a way he hadn't been in her memories for a long time.

Her chest ached. Not just for Winnie, but for her dad too. She hadn't thought of him in so long, it startled her how sharply the grief returned, like a half-healed scar she'd forgotten was still tender.

She squeezed her eyes shut and turned away before her emotions could completely overtake her. What she needed was rest, no more strikes to her heart or being dragged down memory lane. Spotting the most grandmotherly afghan she'd ever seen draped over the armrest of the couch, she pulled it up over her entire body and even her head, curled into a small ball, and let herself drift away from the weight of this long, terrible day.

***

Bang.

A MURDER MOST UNSOLVED

Freddie's eyes flew open. The sound had come from the bookstore. A thud, then something shifting faintly, but enough to wake her from a dead sleep.

Aggie's ears were perked up from his resting spot, curled at Freddie's feet.

Freddie, followed closely by Aggie, crept down the hallway, her heartbeat quickening. She paused at the secret door, cracked it open just enough to peek through.

An older man stood in the middle of the store.

He was dressed in a tailored brown coat, his silver hair slightly disheveled. He was browsing the shelves with a slow, deliberate motion—pulling books off, flipping through them, then returning them absently. His brow furrowed in contemplation.

Freddie watched as he turned toward the display case at the front of the store, Winnie's shrine to *Father Grey*. DVDs, vintage posters, and an autographed photo in a dusty gold frame. Most people never noticed the actor's signature until Winnie pointed it out to them, which she did frequently.

The man stared at it for a long time, a smile stretching from ear to ear.

Then she saw it just as she stepped through the doorway. The profile. The eyebrows. The voice, when he finally spoke.

"Oh hello," he said with a gentle British lilt. "I'm looking for Winifred March. She'd written me a letter asking me to visit. I'm—"

"—Nigel Ashcroft," Freddie said, stunned, stepping into the light. Her voice was barely a whisper.

He straightened, his eyes narrowing slightly.

"Yes," he said after a pause, offering a slight bow. "I see my reputation precedes me."

5

FATHER GREY

Father Grey had always been Winnie's favorite television show.

Freddie never quite understood why, at least not as a child. It was slow, talky, and everyone seemed to wear the same drab tweed jackets in every episode except *Father Grey*, of course. He always wore his black, flowing cassock and carried his long umbrella, which served to protect him from rain but also as a doorstop, a weapon, or for any other clever purpose when needed. But it had been on a constant loop at The Marple & Quill, on the little boxy TV in Winnie's back apartment, the one with bunny ears wrapped in tinfoil. And when Freddie moved away, she found herself tuning in to the reruns that played late at night on the British station she got through her minimal cable package.

She now knew every episode by heart and could quote entire scenes. And even if she still rolled her eyes at the over-the-top dialogue or the oddly convenient clue reveals, *Father Grey* had become something else entirely.

A connection.

To Winnie.

To childhood.

To a person who had loved her without question, even when she couldn't bring herself to pick up the phone or buy a plane ticket.

Freddie had grown to love *Father Grey*. Not just for its campy British wit, but because it made her feel something she hadn't felt in years. Close. To someone. To anyone.

Her life in the city had become narrow. Quiet. Most days were spent alone in the library archives, poring over dusty documents no one cared about. Evenings were the same, lonely: takeout containers, late-night reading, maybe an old movie for company. She had no real friends. No boyfriend. Her mother had died when she was nineteen, and after that, Freddie stopped trying to build bridges. Her heart just couldn't take watching those bridges burn any longer.

The only tether she had left to the world was the stack of letters exchanged with Winnie over the years; pages and pages of memories, book recommendations, town gossip, and sharp, scribbled love.

But they weren't enough. Not really.

She hadn't seen Winnie in person since she was ten. And now she never would.

Her thoughts were broken by Nigel's voice, soft and uncertain.

"So she died? Today?" he asked, after a long pause while he contemplated the news. "That just doesn't seem possible. I mean, it is possible, obviously. Just... a strange turn of events that she'd die on the exact day I arrive."

"Me too," Freddie said, her voice hollow. "I just got here today too."

Before either of them could say more, the shop's bell jingled above the door.

Pru stepped inside with a plastic tub of baked goods in her arms and froze mid-step. Her eyes widened as they locked onto Nigel Ashcroft standing in front of the *Father Grey* display.

Her mouth opened slightly.

Then, in a voice several octaves higher than usual, she said, "Well, butter my biscuit!"

Nigel blinked. "Pardon?"

"You're—you're him! Nigel Ashcroft. *Father Grey*." She dropped the baked goods on the nearest table. "Oh, my word, Winnie and I watched your show religiously. We had a whole tradition. Tea, shortbread, and British murder. Every Thursday night. I even kicked Kevin out of the kitchen and made him watch the Christmas special with a paper crown on."

Nigel offered a polite smile. "That's very kind."

"I had the biggest crush on you." Pru gave a laugh, equal parts embarrassment and delight. "Not on the priest, obviously. That would've been weird. But on you. The actor version. Winnie says you look like a man who could find a body and bake a scone before noon." Her words put Winnie still in the present tense; then she caught herself, flinched, and smoothed her apron.

"Well," Nigel said with mock modesty, "she isn't entirely wrong, I suppose."

Pru turned to Freddie, her expression still giddy. "You didn't tell me he was in the bookstore!"

"I didn't know," Freddie said. "I just, well...found him here."

Nigel scratched the back of his neck sheepishly. "Winnie invited me. Said she had theatrical connections she wanted to introduce me to. These days, I suppose I could use all the help I can get," he added, embarrassment fringing his words.

Pru paused, blinked, and let out a short, surprised laugh. "Winnie? Theatrical connections? Unless she meant Rupert down at the Fernridge Community Theatre, whose last production of *Arsenic and Old Lace* nearly set the basement on fire; well, bless her, but Winnie's idea of the industry was a twenty-year-old DVD player."

Nigel looked genuinely confused. "But... her letter. She said she was sick and it was her final wish to meet me and introduce me to her theatre connections to help my career. She said she was gravely ill. I assumed she was in hospice. That she—"

"She wasn't," Pru said firmly with a little stomp of her foot. "Winifred March was about as far from ill as a woman could be. She was sharp, snarky, and full of too much cinnamon and conspiracy to slow down."

Nigel frowned, fumbling in his coat pocket, then his bag. "I have the letter. Somewhere. She wrote to me. Invited me here. Told me she had a connection I needed to meet. That she was dying. That it was her final wish."

Freddie felt a chill tighten in her spine.

"She wrote to me too," she said quietly.

Both Nigel and Pru looked at her.

Freddie pulled the wrinkled paper from her pants pocket and unfolded it slowly, reading it again as if it might make more sense now than it did the day before yesterday when it arrived.

You must come back to Fernridge. It's a matter of life and death. Don't tell anyone. Just come back home. Please, Freddie.

She looked up, her voice soft and broken. "She wrote this. Said I had to come immediately. And now... she's gone. I don't understand."

Silence settled over the group.

Outside, the sun had started to set behind the hills, casting long shadows through the windows.

Inside, the bookstore suddenly felt a little colder.

6

LET IT STAY BURIED

The bell above the Bloom Room flower shop door jingled as Freddie and Pru stepped inside. The air was thick with the sweetness of lilies and roses, it was almost too much after the sterile smell and hushed chill of the funeral home they had just left. The funeral home was much quicker than Freddie had imagined. The funeral home director, Sid, said Freddie had already made all the necessary arrangements years ago and had even finished the payments, so there really wasn't much left to do. Sid had set everything in motion the minute he heard of her death. It all seemed too easy to Freddie, and she found it unsettling how quickly and neatly things had been wrapped up and secured with a bow.

Now at the flower shop, stems rustled in their vases like restless guests, and the counter overflowed with ribbon, shears, and florist wire. A small dog slept curled up in its tiny dog bed at the end of the counter with flower stems discarded all around it. Freddie saw it all, but the morning was passing by her quickly, and also in a complete haze. She couldn't seem to shake the numbness she felt at having to arrange her grandmother's funeral upon just arriving back in Fernridge.

Sylvia Bloom, the owner of the Bloom Room, looked up from an arrangement of white roses, her auburn hair twisted into a bun that was coming loose in a way that seemed more intentional than due to a hard day's work. She wore a dark blue apron streaked with pollen, and her smile came just a half-second late.

"Well, well. Fernridge's busiest women," she said toward Pru, her voice smooth but carrying something just sharp enough to snag. "Come to check my work for the funeral?"

"Not check," Pru replied quickly, her tone light but firm. "Just making sure things are set for tomorrow."

Sylvia arched a brow. "Of course. Winifred deserves nothing but the best." She slid another rose into the vase with unnecessary precision. "I'd already arranged for extra lilies—though I suppose you'd know how she preferred her flowers, wouldn't you, Prudence? You know everything after all."

Pru's jaw tightened, but she didn't look away. "Lilies wilt too fast. Hydrangeas will last through the service."

Freddie glanced between them, feeling the temperature dip. "Everything looks beautiful," she offered, hoping to soften the moment. "Winnie would've loved all of this."

Sylvia's smile didn't reach her eyes. "She always did have impeccable taste. A rare quality these days."

Pru crossed her arms, her voice bright but edged. "Funny, that's exactly what Kal used to say."

Freddie blinked, unsure she'd heard right, but Sylvia's lips curved into something comparable to an evil grin. "Kal always appreciated beauty when he saw it." She leaned closer to Freddie, lowering her voice conspiratorially. "Your grandmother must've been so proud to have such loyal friends."

Freddie managed a polite nod, though confusion was what she really felt.

Sylvia turned back to her roses, clipping a stem with a crisp snap that sent the stem flying over to near where the dog still lay sleeping. "The arrangements will be delivered first thing in the morning. You can trust me on that." Her tone made it sound like a dare more than reassurance.

"Good," Pru said shortly, spinning on her heel. "We'll see you tomorrow."

Freddie hurried behind Pru and finally caught up with her on the sidewalk. "What was that about? Did I miss something?"

Pru exhaled hard, shoving her hands into her pockets. "Sylvia Bloom is what happened. My husband, Kal? He walked out on me years ago—for her. Didn't last, of course, the only thing that Sylvia sticks to is her flowers. Things that remove themselves are usually better left forgotten." She shrugged, though her eyes stayed hard. "But Sylvia never could resist reminding me."

Freddie stayed quiet, still processing, as they walked back toward the bookstore. Another piece of Fernridge's puzzle, thornier than flowers should ever be.

***

A MURDER MOST UNSOLVED

In the wee hours that night, Freddie couldn't sleep, and she really needed a Diet Coke. Winnie had every flavor of tea imaginable, but not a single can of Diet Coke.

The sun hadn't risen yet, but the sky was already softening at the edges, casting a bluish glow through the bookstore windows. The Marple & Quill was eerily quiet this early in the morning. Even Aggie, usually a purring sentinel at her feet, had taken up post somewhere in the stacks.

Freddie sat cross-legged in front of a shelf she hadn't paid much attention to before: cookbooks. Or at least, that's what the label claimed. Above the section, a tiny stained-glass skylight window cast ruby, amber, and moss-colored squares of light over the spines, which shifted when a breeze nudged the old building.

She wasn't looking for comfort food. She wasn't even sure what she was doing, really. She just needed something to do to make the hours pass faster between now and the funeral. Something that didn't require standing still with her thoughts. So there she was, just aimlessly walking along the stacks. The floorboards creaked in familiar patterns, like the shop itself had a voice.

She was about to give up and move on when her hand knocked against the back of the shelf. It thudded. Not the hollow wooden sound she expected, but a dull thump like something was behind it.

She frowned, leaned in, and pressed her palm flat. There was a seam.

Of course. Winnie had always loved secret compartments and hidden drawers. Once, she'd hollowed out a copy of *Murder on the Orient Express* just to hide the good chocolate.

Freddie carefully pulled the false backing loose and reached behind it. Her fingers closed around something papery and stiff.

She tugged it free to find a large manila folder, warped slightly at the corners, and secured with a string of faded ribbon. A bunch of loose papers was stuffed inside, along with what appeared to be a massive sheet of paper, folded several times and yellowed with age and use.

Freddie hesitated for a moment. Then opened it.

What spilled out onto the floor was... chaos.

Pages of notes in Winnie's familiar handwriting, a hand-drawn map of Fernridge complete with squiggly lines and confusing arrows, and at the center of it all was a thick, crumpled manila envelope with a wax seal. One page bore a perfect tea ring and the notation: *NEVER MAKE RASPBERRY SCONES AGAIN* underlined three times. Winnie's scribblings in her book margins had always been part lecture, part gossip: *NEVER TRUST A BUTLER NAMED BARRY*; *Mrs. Halpern owes me a pie tin*.

She scanned the loose notes, heart pounding harder the more she read.

Timeline of sightings: May to July Church bell repair — confirmed 1998

Another page:

Left leg drag

Stutters under pressure

Sightings: twice outside bakery, once near church.

At first, she blinked, trying to make sense of the scrawl. It wasn't just Winnie's usual ramblings, like the multitude of Post-it notes she'd found stuck all over the bookstore and apartment. There was a pattern, a purpose.

And at the very bottom of the worst-drawn timeline Freddie had ever seen were words, circled in red ink:

A MURDER MOST UNSOLVED

Father Grey Episode 10x6 A Murder Most Unsolved

Freddie sucked in a breath.

She thought she knew that one. It was quite a well-known episode.

It was the only episode that ended with more questions than answers; the killer was hinted at but never revealed. Winnie had always called it "the one that got away."

She picked up the folded spiral page. There were only a few lines.

Real murder IN Fernridge. Victim??? – unknown (death ~19 years ago) How Nigel involved?

No further context. Just those cryptic words, written in Winnie's hand.

Freddie's fingers tightened around the paper.

She wanted to laugh. Or cry. Or crumple the whole pile into a ball and shove it back behind the cookbooks. This was absurd. Winnie always had a flair for the dramatic but surely this was just her turning real events into a fictional puzzle. Something to pass the time.

But something in Freddie's gut told her it wasn't that simple.

Especially not with what she remembered from that episode: a person found dead with a cup of tea and a book in their lap. A man with a limp and a stutter who vanished before anyone could question him.

And here was Winnie. Found in her favorite chair. Tea in hand. Book open.

Freddie sat back, stunned.

She didn't want to believe what her brain was telling her.

Did someone murder her grandmother?

She looked back at the mess of papers scattered across the floor.

No.

Not yet. She wasn't ready to say that out loud.

Not until she knew for sure.

She carefully gathered the pages, returned them to the folder, and slipped it into her bag.

She would go to the funeral. She would say goodbye.

And then she'd find out what Winnie had started.

But for now, she would keep it to herself.

7

A Dish of Memory

Freddie hadn't expected a crowd.

She'd pictured something small, just a handful of people huddled around a headstone. But as her car turned into the narrow gravel lane that wound through Fernridge Cemetery, her stomach flipped.

The crowd spilled far beyond the neat circle of folding chairs set up near the grave. People stood in clusters under magnolia trees and along the fence line, voices low, faces somber. It looked like half the county had turned out. Men in pastel suits fanned themselves while women in wide-brimmed hats whispered, *"She once snuck me a romance novel—don't tell Harold."*

She was sure there were more people here than the entire population of Fernridge.

When she stepped out of the car, the hum of conversation softened, heads turning toward her. She tried to weave her way through the swarm of bodies, murmuring "Excuse me" in a voice that went unheard.

Then, from somewhere ahead, a sharp whistle cut through the air.

"Make way for the granddaughter!" Pru's voice rang clear. The crowd shifted instantly, creating a path down the middle like Moses parting the Red Sea.

As Freddie made her way through the mourners, she noticed the florist weaving through the rows of chairs. Sylvia Bloom's hair was pinned back too tightly, and her cheeks were flushed with beads of sweat pooling on her upper lip. She carried a box of extra ribbons in one hand and a pair of shears in the other, like a general stalking the field of battle.

"Oh, for heaven's sake," Sylvia muttered, crouching by a spray of lilies at the foot of the casket. "The bow's slipped again. Amateur work. If I'd had more time..." Her voice trailed off as she adjusted the ribbon, but not before Pru stiffened beside Freddie.

"Looks fine to me," Pru said, her tone light but her jaw set.

Sylvia glanced up, eyes narrowing just slightly. "Of course it does. You always did prefer...rustic." She straightened, smoothing her skirt.

Pru's smile was sharp as a pastry cutter. "Better rustic than artificial."

Freddie blinked between them, caught in the static hum of their tension. "Everything looks beautiful," she said quickly, hoping to defuse the moment. "Winnie would've loved it."

Sylvia's expression softened only for Freddie. "She had excellent taste. Always insisted on fresh-cut. Nothing cheap." Then, as she turned to leave, she gave Pru one last pointed look. "I suppose some standards never change."

Pru didn't respond until Sylvia was out of earshot. Then she exhaled hard through her nose, muttering, "Standards, my left foot."

Freddie's cheeks flushed, but she kept moving until she reached the edge of the graveside, where a tall man in a black cassock stood waiting.

Father Keating, the town's priest, stepped forward, hands folded over a worn Bible. He gave Freddie a somber and knowing nod, then spoke. His voice carried easily, smooth and warm.

"Good morning, everyone. We are here today to remember Winifred March and celebrate her glorious life," he began. "A woman of great generosity, quick wit, and boundless spirit. She gave as freely of her time as she did of her books and scones. She was kind—but she was also ornery when the occasion called, which was, in her opinion, quite often."

The crowd chuckled softly, and Father Keating's mouth curved in a fond smile.

"She loved this town," he went on. "And this town loved her back. She was the keeper of stories—not just the ones on her shelves, but the ones in our hearts. We will miss her laugh, her sharp opinions on mystery novels, and the way she made each of us feel we mattered."

Freddie's throat tightened. His words pressed heavily against her chest, each one a reminder of the years she'd stayed away. The letters she'd written instead of visiting. The birthdays missed. The afternoons that would never come again. In the city, funerals were brief and polite; here, grief looked like a potluck with a sermon, every person adding a dish of memory.

And yet, everyone spoke as though Winnie had been full of life right up until the end. Strong. Healthy. A woman with plans still left to make. Not someone fading away.

The thought slid uninvited into Freddie's mind: *Someone killed her.*

A shiver ran through her.

When the service ended, people began approaching her and shaking her hand, patting her arm, and offering soft words.

"She was the best neighbor I ever had," said a tall, thin man who smelled faintly of mothballs.

Freddie's hand was swallowed in a large, warm grip. "Sorry for your loss," the man said, his voice low and careful. She noticed a faint hitch in his step as he moved aside to let an older woman pass. "Old injury," he added quickly, as if reading her mind. "Took a bad fall back in the day." His smile was quick yet polite, but his eyes didn't linger.

Her attention turned to a severe-looking woman with tiny, black eyes who croaked through a frog in her throat, "She kept me in tea and biscuits all last winter when I couldn't get to town." She turned away as she dabbed her teary eyes.

Another person pushed forward. "I sure hope you'll keep the bookstore open. Fernridge wouldn't be the same without it," said a young twenty-something whose face was red from tears.

Freddie forced a small smile, nodding. "Thank you. That's... kind."

They just kept coming, townsperson after townsperson. It went on for what felt like hours. She didn't like the recognition and thought she didn't deserve the kind words that were really meant for her grandmother. A woman she had all but abandoned. She moved to the edge of the crowd, trying her best to escape them.

Then she felt it, eyes staring daggers through her, and another chill went down her back.

She glanced up and saw a man, the man who shook her hand earlier, standing several rows back, near an old row of headstones mottled with lichen. He was staring at her, unblinking. When their eyes met, his mouth twitched into something between a smirk and a scowl. Then he turned and limped behind a tall gravestone.

He limped. Not a slight limp like earlier, but an odd, dragging hitch in his left leg. A limp like Winnie had written in her notes.

Freddie's pulse spiked.

She edged away from the group pressing in on her, murmuring apologies, trying to keep him in sight. If she could just hear him speak more, just see if there was a stutter, maybe she'd know if he was the man Winnie had written about.

But by the time she reached the row of headstones where she'd lost sight of him, he was gone.

She scanned the cemetery. Nothing. No trace of him. She turned quickly on her heels, still searching the far off distance for any sight of the limping man, and bumped into a person with a thud.

"Ah...so sorry, I didn't see you there."

She looked up sharply, from her new resting spot on the ground, to find Nigel Ashcroft standing a few feet away, reaching a hand out to help her off the ground and looking far too eager for someone at a funeral. "I had been hoping to speak with you, but I wasn't planning on literally bumping into you," he said, smoothing the lapel of his suit jacket. "I'd like to come by the bookstore to talk before you leave town."

Freddie eyed him, her thoughts snapping to Winnie's note and the timeline she'd found. Nigel was the credited writer of *A Murder Most Unsolved*. The only unsolved *Father Grey* episode. He had arrived in Fernridge the very same day Winnie died.

She gave him a little nod of agreement but didn't speak.

Nigel leaned in, lowering his voice. "Strange, isn't it? Funerals. You always notice the people you don't expect to see."

Freddie blinked. "What do you mean?"

"Oh... nothing," he said dismissively, smoothing his lapel once again. "Only that Fernridge seems full of surprises and maybe some hidden ghosts. We'll speak more later." He said as he waved a little goodbye and turned to leave.

Her suspicion curled like smoke in her mind.

And for the first time, she admitted the word she'd been avoiding: *murder.*

She was certain of it now. Winifred March, her Winnie, had been murdered.

And this Winifred March was going to find out who had done it.

8

THE KEEPER OF STORIES

The magnolia blossoms swayed gently in the warm afternoon breeze as the last of the mourners trickled away. Freddie stood near the gravel path, staring down at her shoes, half-listening to Pru's gentle instructions about "next steps" after a funeral. She wasn't sure if Pru was talking about casseroles or emotional recovery. Maybe both.

"Come on," Pru said at last, looping her arm through Freddie's. "We're going back to the bookstore. No arguments. I've got fresh peach turnovers cooling on the counter, and you look like you haven't eaten in a week. Kevin will drive your rental car back for you. I think you could do with a little walk to help clear your head."

Kevin stood there with his hand out, ready to accept her keys. He was in his mid-twenties, with brown hair and brown eyes, and a nice, calming smile. He appeared to be a very average individual. But Freddie knew that Pru depended on him to assist her with almost everything in life, which made him anything but average.

Freddie didn't resist. She was too busy glancing over her shoulder, scanning the thinning crowd, but the limping man was gone. No sign of his dark coat, his pale face, that strange smirk. Had she imagined it? No. The memory of his dragging left leg was etched in her mind as clearly as the words in Winnie's notes.

The walk back to The Marple & Quill took them past Fernridge's neat rows of brick-front shops. Pru seemed to know every single person they passed, calling out greetings, exchanging quick hugs, and accepting a jar of pickled okra from a woman in a sun hat. It was like moving through a living web of connections, every thread tied to Winnie in some way. Freddie felt herself both tethered to it and hovering awkwardly at the edge.

When they reached the bookstore, Pru pushed the door open and ushered her inside with a little flourish. "I know it feels impossible right now," Pru said, "but this place? It's still yours. And it's still magic. You'll see." She gave Freddie a knowing wink.

The air inside was warm with the scent of cinnamon, fresh flowers, and books. Pru had lit the reading lamps, set a small bouquet of daisies by the register, and filled the bakery display with golden scones and sugar-dusted turnovers. The broken teacups were gone, the scattered books reshelved. It looked back to normal, and Freddie thought it was extraordinary.

Almost.

Sitting in one of the wingback chairs near the front was Nigel Ashcroft, legs crossed, hands folded on the head of his umbrella like a stage prop. Two women in quilted vests perched on the sofa opposite him, hanging on his every word as he recounted, with grand hand gestures, the perils of filming in the Scottish Highlands during a "particularly moody" fog.

When he saw Freddie, his expression brightened as though they were old friends. "Ah! Miss March. Just the person I was hoping to see." He rose, with surprising agility for a man of his affected stiffness, and offered a bow so slight it might have been a nod. "I wanted to extend my condolences again. Your grandmother was, by all accounts, extraordinary."

"Thank you," Freddie said cautiously. Her mind immediately replayed Winnie's note: **How Nigel involved?**

Nigel's gaze flickered with something she couldn't name. "I hear she had a remarkable instinct for a good mystery. Sharp mind. Always asking questions others wouldn't dare. In fact, from everyone's stories I believe she reminded me a great deal of *Father Grey* himself." He chuckled softly. "I hear she had a great interest in the... ah... unique nature of my tenth season finale. And I see she has it in prime display in the window." He gestured toward the *Father Grey* display.

Freddie's heart ticked faster. "You mean *A Murder Most Unsolved*?"

His smile deepened. "You know it, then." Before she could answer, one of the quilted-vest ladies touched his arm, asking about his "favorite case." He gave Freddie a parting nod and turned back to them, his voice slipping into another polished anecdote.

Pru watched him for a moment before leaning in close to Freddie. "You've got that look."

"What look?" Freddie asked, a little too quickly at her potential accusation.

"The one you get right before you go sticking your nose somewhere dangerous. I've seen it before. Usually ends with you getting grounded... or someone threatening to ban you from the bake sale. Winnie had it too."

Freddie's lips twitched despite herself. "I'm just... thinking."

"Uh-huh." Pru's eyes narrowed, but she didn't push. "Well, when you're done thinking, eat one of those turnovers before Nigel eats them all."

Before Freddie could answer, the front bell jingled again. Two women stepped inside, still in their funeral dresses. One made a beeline for the display of new fiction, the other for the pastries.

"We thought we'd stop in," the first woman said, her voice a little thick. "We wanted to support the shop today. For Winnie."

Within minutes, more mourners followed. A retired teacher buying poetry "because Winnie would insist on it." A young man in overalls looking for something "funny, but still with heart, like Winnie." A pair of sisters who ordered half a dozen scones "for the road."

Freddie blinked at them all, startled by the sudden energy. Pru didn't miss a beat—she grabbed her phone and called Kevin. "Bring over pastries—whatever we've got. And a carafe of coffee. We've got a crowd."

While Kevin made the delivery, Pru stationed herself at the counter, showing Freddie how to ring up sales, wrap books in brown paper, and use the industrial-sized coffee maker for needed refills. "And if you're not sure where something is, just point them to the armchair and tell them to take a seat," she said. "Nobody minds waiting when they've got a good view of the front window."

It worked. The hum of conversation and the clink of coffee cups filled the shop. Freddie found herself handing over a wrapped romance novel with a smile, then helping a little girl in patent leather shoes pick out a picture book about a ballerina.

"I want to dance like her," the girl whispered, clutching the book to her chest.

"I think you will," Freddie said, and meant it.

A teenage girl lingered by the mystery section, looking uncertain. Freddie picked up a well-loved paperback. "This one was my first. A classic locked-room mystery. You'll guess the wrong person at least twice."

The girl's face lit up. "I'll take it."

Somewhere between the coffee pours, the laughter, and the small moments of connection, Freddie felt a soft warmth spread through her chest. Warmer than her usual cup of Earl Grey. Warmer, even, than Aggie curling into her lap.

She'd loved her archives job for its order and solitude, but this, this was different. Here, she was part of something alive. Something that breathed with the town's own rhythm. The keeper of stories, a highly regarded position she thought.

Upstairs that evening, Freddie finally pulled Winnie's manila folder from her bag. She spread the notes out on the table again: the timelines, the map, and the lists of sightings. She added her own neat scrawl to the margin: **Funeral — man with limp. Hitch in left leg. Watched me.** She hesitated, then underlined **Watched me** twice.

From the street below came the faint murmur of a voice and the creak of a door stopped by a deadbolt. Freddie moved to the window, peering out through the lace curtain. Across the street, a figure was moving quickly toward the alley, too far to see clearly, but the gait was uneven, the left leg dragging ever so slightly.

Her pulse jumped.

The figure vanished into a shadow.

Freddie's grip tightened on the curtain. "If you were murdered, Winnie," she whispered, "I'm going to prove it."

9

THE BELL TOWER

Freddie woke before dawn, the first blush of light spilling through the bookstore's upstairs window. The air was cool, still holding the night's hush. She lay on the couch, staring at the ceiling, Winnie's folder still spread open on the coffee table.

Her eyes drifted again to the page with the limping man's description: **Left leg drags. Stutters under pressure. Sightings twice outside the bakery, once near the church.**

She tapped the pen against the paper, chewing her lip. She'd spent all night telling herself she'd imagined the man in the cemetery. That it was just her brain latching onto a coincidence. But now, with Winnie's notes staring back at her, it felt like willful blindness to ignore it.

Freddie wasn't a detective. She wasn't even good at board game mysteries, which is why everyone always beat her at *Clue*. But she was good at digging, at piecing together scraps of information until a pattern appeared. And Winnie's folder was begging to be completed.

She grabbed her bag, tucking the folder inside. "Alright, Fernridge," she muttered, "let's see what you're hiding."

A MURDER MOST UNSOLVED

The first stop on her tour of clues in Winnie's notes was the church. It sat at the far end of Main Street, its white steeple catching the sunrise like a beacon. The paint on the steps was peeling in tidy strips, as though even its decay preferred to be orderly.

Freddie hesitated at the door before pushing it open. The sanctuary was quiet, smelling faintly of burning candles and incense. A slant of light from the stained glass cast jewel tones across the polished floorboards. She was on the hunt to speak to the Father.

Father Thomas Keating was in his early sixties, though Fernridge's gossip mill insisted he was both older and younger depending on who you asked. He had a solid build that came more from years of lifting hymnals, church chairs, and casseroles than from any exercise regimen. His face was broad and kind, weathered in a way that suggested a life of listening more than speaking. Fine laugh lines feathered out from his eyes, which were a clear, thoughtful gray that seemed to see both the surface of things and just beneath them.

His hair, once thick and black, had faded to a dignified silver at the temples, kept neatly trimmed though it had a stubborn wave that resisted perfect order. His clerical collar always looked crisp, but his shirtsleeves were nearly always rolled up, as though he'd just come from fixing a leaky faucet or carrying folding tables. He smelled faintly of candle wax, strong tea, and old books.

When he walked, there was a steady weight to his stride—not heavy, but grounded, like a man who had spent decades moving slowly through rooms where grief and joy coexisted.

There was nothing flashy about him, and yet people gravitated toward his presence. His voice carried the soft authority of someone who could quiet a room without ever raising his tone. And when he laughed, which was more often than he let on, it had a warmth that could make the most skeptical soul believe in small miracles again.

Father Keating emerged from a side room, rolling up his shirtsleeves per usual. His face lit with recognition. "Miss March. Didn't expect to see you here so soon after yesterday."

"I had, well, a question," Freddie said, trying to sound casual. "Winnie's notes mentioned the church bell being repaired back in '98. Do you know anything about that?"

He gave her a mild smile, the kind that didn't give anything away. "Ah, yes. A terrible storm that summer, and lightning struck the tower. The old mechanism was damaged beyond repair. We had to replace it entirely. Cost the parish a small fortune."

He stepped into the light, resting his hands on the back of the nearest bench. "Why do you ask?"

Freddie hesitated. "Just curious, really. She seemed to think it mattered, and I'm just trying to piece her life here together."

"Your grandmother loved her stories," he said, the corners of his mouth twitching in something between fondness and caution. "Sometimes she'd make a mystery out of a pothole in the road, though."

Freddie tilted her head. "Did anyone get hurt that year? Maybe someone who worked on the repair crew?"

Father Keating's hands shifted, one sliding over the other. "There were a few minor mishaps. Work at that height is never without risk." He adjusted his cuffs, though they were already neatly rolled. "One man, a local, I think, fell from the scaffolding but survived. Shook him up badly, though. I can't recall his name."

A MURDER MOST UNSOLVED

"You don't remember?" she asked, her disappointment showing a little too much.

"Names fade, Miss March. The years blur together when you've officiated hundreds of weddings, even more funerals, and heard more confessions than one could attempt to count." He glanced toward the far wall, where a narrow ladder led up to the belfry. "Perhaps you should check the town archives at the library if you're so inclined. Records don't forget like people do." He tapped his temple for emphasis.

Freddie thought that sounded like a great idea; after all, she could do library research in her sleep.

As she turned to leave, Father Keating added, "The bell rang again in time for the Summer Festival that year. Winnie was so pleased, she said it was like the town's heartbeat returning." His voice softened on the last phrase, but when she glanced back, he was already moving toward the altar, his expression unreadable.

The Fernridge Public Library was two blocks over, housed in what had once been the town's post office. Although it was aging, the building was a grand testament to early 20th-century Art Deco architecture. Even in the vast space, the scent of old paper hit her the moment she stepped in, richer and less dusty than The Marple & Quill; here, the books seemed to have been quietly napping for decades.

The librarian, a brisk woman in a sweater vest, pointed her toward the basement archives with the same tone one might use for "the mop closet's down the hall."

Downstairs, rows of metal filing cabinets and bound newspapers lined the walls. Freddie easily found the 1998 editions of the *Fernridge*

Gazette, someone here was very organized, she thought with appreciation as she started to lay them out on the large table.

July: "Lightning Damages Church Bell." August: "Bell Tower Restored Ahead of Summer Festival."

On the next page, a small column caught her eye: *Man injured in construction mishap. John Doe hospitalized after fall from scaffolding during church repairs. Condition stable.*

No follow-up. No photo. No name.

She leaned closer, tracing the grainy ink with her finger, willing it to give her more information.

Footsteps creaked overhead. Nothing unusual, until they grew louder. Then softer. Then stopped.

Freddie froze, glancing toward the stairwell.

A shadow passed along the narrow strip of light under the door.

Her heart thudded. She took a cautious step toward the stairs just in time to catch a figure moving past the frosted glass window. The outline was blurred, but the gait was unmistakable: the odd, dragging hitch of a left leg. If it wasn't so exaggerated in the movement, Freddie might believe she was imagining the awkward gait on every innocent passerby; however, it was tough to mistake.

"Hey!" she called as she found a little bit of courage buried deep, though her voice shakier than intended.

The shadow momentarily paused, but then moved quickly out of sight.

Freddie bolted up the stairs, taking them two at a time, but by the time she reached the main floor, the front door stood open to the morning breeze. The street outside was empty.

Freddie lingered a moment longer at the edge of the library entrance, scanning for any sign of movement. Nothing.

She turned back toward the main path, ready to head for the bookstore and froze. A voice, low and deliberate, carried from the street over.

Nigel's voice.

She couldn't make out every word, just fragments: "…no, not yet… of course I remember… yes, but that's not what." A pause. Then a sharp, almost irritated, "I said I'll handle it."

Freddie's pulse kicked up.

She took a cautious step toward the corner, straining to hear more, but the sound cut off abruptly. When she rounded the corner, the narrow lane was empty except for Nigel himself, strolling toward her with his usual polished smile.

"Ah, Miss March!" he called, as if they'd merely bumped into each other. "I was just admiring the architecture. Rather Gothic, isn't it?"

If there had been someone else with him, they were gone now.

Freddie tried to keep her expression neutral, but her mind was turning over fast. "Right. Gothic," she said as they both looked up at the library walls.

Nigel's gaze flickered, just for a second, down the street in the direction he'd just come. Then he smoothed his lapel, his tone brightening almost too much. "Shall I walk you back to the bookstore?"

As they walked side by side, Freddie kept stealing glances at him, her thoughts circling like crows over a field. *The limping man. Nigel's voice, low and urgent. Who had he been talking to? Was he connected to the limping man? And that single, unshakable thought: both of them were here, in Fernridge, the day Winnie died.*

Back at the shop, she spread out Winnie's notes and added a new line to the timeline. **Day after funeral—spotted at library, same limp**

She closed the folder with a snap. Whoever this man was, he wasn't just a ghost from Winnie's old research. He was here, and she was sure he was watching her. And Nigel seemed to always appear around the same time as him. She wasn't sure what the connection was, if there even was one, but she'd find out.

And for the first time since arriving in Fernridge, Freddie felt something other than grief.

Purpose.

She whispered it out loud, tasting the word: "Investigation."

Then, almost smiling, she added, "You picked the wrong granddaughter to scare."

10

THE PIE & POETRY PICNIC

By midmorning, Fernridge had unfolded into the kind of day that made postcards jealous. The sky was a ridiculous blue, a choir of cicadas buzzed somewhere in the trees, and the town square had transformed into a quilt of picnic blankets and lawn chairs for the Pie & Poetry Picnic.

Pru had insisted. "It's a civic duty," she'd declared, thrusting a lemon tart into Freddie's hands as if it were her passport. "People remember who shows up and who doesn't."

So Freddie showed up. She even brought paper plates.

The lawn was dotted with card tables draped in gingham. Kids skittered past with lemonade cups, and a trio of elderly women in matching cardigans that were embroidered with tiny knitting needles and skulls, sat in stern judgment beside a pie judging sign that read: **NO BRIBES (UNLESS SUBTLE)**.

Freddie looked past the lemonade in search of a Diet Coke. Why was Diet Coke in such short supply in this town? She made a mental note to ask Pru where she could locate a supply.

"Relax your shoulders," Pru murmured, steering Freddie through the cluster of neighbors. "You're hunching like you're about to be graded."

"I might be," Freddie whispered back. "By everyone."

"Welcome to small town living, welcome to Fernridge. Now smile and they'll judge you less." She prodded playfully.

They staked out a patch of shade under a magnolia. Kevin appeared like a harried bumblebee, wearing a **TEAM PRU** apron and carrying forks. "You're up in twenty minutes," he told Pru. "Cherry lattice has cooled. I repeated the crimp on the edge like you like it."

"Bless you, Kevin. If we win, I'll put your name on the chalkboard in swirlies."

"If we win," he said, already backing away, "I want a raise."

"Swirlies," Pru repeated, with enthusiasm.

A local beekeeper took the mic and cleared his throat. "Haiku about bees," he announced. "Because the bees asked." He read with solemnity:

Honey hums in jars
Town holds its breath, mouths ready—
Winnie's honey scones.

The crowd made a soft, collective sound that was not quite a laugh and not quite a sigh. Freddie felt it under her ribs as she tried to hold in a laugh.

A familiar voice floated over the lawn: "—and that's how we staged the rain for the Christmas special—"

Nigel Ashcroft had found a chair near the lemonade stand and was entertaining a semicircle of admirers. He looked more rumpled than yesterday, as if the day had begun with equal parts grooming and regret, but he was in good voice and better spirits. When his eyes met Freddie's across the crowd, he lifted his paper cup in a toast and offered a small smile. Pru lifted her brow and mouthed, *behave*, then proceeded to fluff her hair.

"Don't," Freddie murmured, not wanting Pru to get any more *involved* with Nigel yet knowing that's exactly where Pru was hoping things would go.

"I would never," Pru said, already half gone in Nigel's direction. "If anyone asks, I'm networking."

Freddie wandered toward the pie tables. Every dessert looked like an argument for staying in Fernridge: peach with sugared tops, blueberry with star cutouts, pecan crammed with more pecans than should be legal. A woman in a wide hat stared with ferocious concentration at a meringue, as if it might confess who overwhipped it.

Two older women stood on the other side of the table, voices pitched just low enough to pretend they weren't gossiping.

"...came back a few months ago," one said, adjusting her brooch. "Late nights. Keeps to himself."

The other sniffed. "Lives over by the old Motor Court. Walks like one leg's asleep, you know."

Freddie's attention snapped into focus. "Sorry, excuse me. I'm new, well, not new, but..." She gave up and just asked what she wanted to know. "Who did you say came back?"

The two women blinked at her in unison. The first one's expression softened. "You're Winifred's granddaughter."

Freddie nodded. "Freddie."

"Bless you, honey." The second woman reached out, patted her wrist once, then looked over each shoulder like the pies might be wired. "It's not our business, is it, Ada?"

"It's never our business," Ada said with the tone of someone who always knew the business. "But if it were our business, and I'm not saying it is, we'd say he's renting near the feed store. Keeps odd hours. You didn't hear it from us."

Freddie willed her voice into casual. "Does he...talk much?"

"Not if he can help it," Ada said. "Stammers when he's forced to converse."

Freddie felt her pulse like a drumroll. "Do you know his name?"

Ada opened her mouth, but the woman with the meringue chose that moment to gasp, "This is collapsing!" and thrust the pie toward them like a medical emergency. By the time Freddie looked back, the two women had migrated toward the lemonade line with the silent efficiency of seasoned escape artists.

"Of course," Freddie muttered. "Just when I was getting some gossip, uh...intel."

She found Pru at the edge of Nigel's circle, pretending not to be dazzled. Nigel was reading, in his crisp stage voice, a poem scrawled on the back of a grocery list:

He never quite speaks
Where the bell refuses time—
A step left behind.

"That's... actually good," Pru whispered. "Infuriating."

Nigel finished to polite applause and bowed in the direction of the lemonade. When he straightened, his eyes flicked again to Freddie. He didn't look theatrical this time. He looked curious. Maybe concerned.

Before she could decide which, Kevin reappeared with a plate and a fork. "Taste," he ordered. "If we lose, I want your last memory to be decent cherry."

Freddie took a bite. The crust shattered delicately; the filling was bright and tart. The taste pinned her to the grass for a second, made of summer and impatience and childhood.

Pru's name was called. She squared her shoulders and advanced toward the judges with the ferocity of a gladiator. Nigel trailed a few paces behind, hands in pockets, as if drawn by the scent of sugar and competition.

"Win this," Freddie murmured to Kevin, "and you get swirlies."

"I don't actually know what that is," he said. "But I'm ready for it."

The poetry continued, a limerick about the feed store chicken that had gotten lost so often it now wore a tag that read *NOT MISSING, JUST MISCHIEVOUS*; an earnest sonnet about the stoplight being installed in 1998 (*"our lone ruby eye to watch the town's small sins"*). Freddie tucked that last bit away. Winnie had circled the stoplight installation on her timeline. Church bell repair and stoplight, same summer. It had once felt like trivia. Now it felt like coordinates. But did the two have anything to do with each other, or was Winnie just looking for connections?

When the judging concluded, Pru returned, face carefully blank. "Well?" Freddie asked.

Pru sniffed. "If I lose to a meringue I'm staging a coup."

They stayed for another hour because everyone stays for another hour: to help stack chairs, to hug people who needed hugging, and to let the day soften around the edges. Nigel drifted over, a little shy at first, like a man reconsidering his angle of approach.

"I hope I didn't intrude," he said. "On the poetry. Or the pies. Or the town." He gave a rueful smile. "I have a talent for arriving uninvited."

"You were invited," Pru said. "By a woman with notoriously good taste in both books and mischief." She lifted her chin toward the magnolia. "And you didn't do half bad with that poem-for-hire."

Nigel's mouth quirked. "It wasn't mine. It was on the community board. I only…arranged it a bit."

His gaze turned to Freddie. "How are you holding up?"

"I'm fine," Freddie said, and then, because she was tired of lying to people she barely knew, "No. Not really."

Nigel nodded like that was the only correct answer. "If I can be of any use…"

Pru slid between them with a smile that was slightly too bright. "You can be of use by helping me carry these pie tins and telling me the story about nearly setting the *Father Grey* set on fire again."

Nigel laughed. "It's better with hand gestures. How about another time?" Then his pace quickened as he walked on ahead.

Freddie fell into step with Pru, pie tin balanced on her forearm, the sun tilting toward late afternoon. She felt it then, startling and simple: she liked this. The air, the chatter, the way everyone seemed to know how to be a person here. It didn't fix anything, and it didn't bring Winnie back, but it made something in her unclench.

They cut down Elder Lane toward The Marple & Quill. The bell over the door gave its cheerful chime when Pru pushed it open, and Aggie emerged from behind the counter with the bored dignity of a shop manager returning from lunch.

"Hi there, sir," Pru said, scratching his chin. "Did you guard the premises?"

Aggie blinked slowly: yes, obviously. Then he hopped onto the front table and sat on a stack of bookmarks like a furry paperweight.

They set the tins behind the counter. Pru went to change the chalkboard sign to **POETRY HANGOVER SPECIAL: BUY TWO COOKIES, GET A COMPLIMENT**.

Freddie stayed by the door and looked at the room the way she had the first day, only now it didn't feel paused. It felt...waiting. She knelt to pick up a stray flyer someone had slid partly under the mat. It was folded once, neatly, the way you fold a note you absolutely want someone to read.

There were only five words, printed in block letters with a thick-tipped pen:

STOP ASKING QUESTIONS. FOR YOUR OWN GOOD.

Freddie's breath went thin.

She turned it over. Nothing. No signature. No flourish. No way to identify the writer.

Pru's laughter from the chalkboard faded as Freddie straightened slowly, the note between her fingers. Aggie stared up at her, tail flicking like a metronome.

"Pru?" Freddie said, and was surprised by the steadiness in her voice. "Could you...come look at this?"

Pru read it once. Twice. She didn't gasp or curse or wring her hands. She simply slid the note into the pocket of her apron and said, very calmly, "Alright. First, we lock the front. Second, we make tea. Third, you tell me what this is about, everything."

Freddie opened her mouth, the reflex to deny, to minimize, to stash this alongside all the other things she hadn't said yet. The reflex passed.

"Okay," she said. "Tea. Then everything."

Pru moved the chalkboard inside, slid the bolt, and set about boiling the kettle like she was arming a cannon.

The day went on being beautiful. The town went on being itself.

And Freddie, who had always been good at keeping secrets, felt the first one loosen in her chest.

She would tell Pru. She would show her Winnie's folder. She would say the word *murder* out loud, in the bright daylight of the shop where everyone came to be human.

And then, together, they would decide what to do next.

11

Everything

Pru's kettle sang like a tiny soprano. She snapped off the flame and poured boiling water over two teabags in fat, floral mugs as if she were mixing medicine.

"Sugar?" she asked, already reaching for the bowl.

"Yes," Freddie said. "A lot."

Pru stirred both, then set the mugs on the table in the little back kitchen of The Marple & Quill. The note from the door, **STOP ASKING QUESTIONS. FOR YOUR OWN GOOD.** lay between them like a third place setting. Pru had been the one to slide it out of her apron and put it back down. "So we can look the bully in the face," she'd said.

Aggie hopped up into a chair, arranged himself like a furry councilman, and fixed Freddie with his yellow stare.

"Alright," Pru said. "Everything."

Freddie exhaled and pulled Winnie's folder from her bag. She untied the faded ribbon and spilled the contents onto the tablecloth: the tea-ringed pages, the terrible map, the jotted lists. Her fingers hovered for a second over the red-circled words before she turned the page so Pru could read.

"*Father Grey*," Pru murmured, eyes skimming. "Of course she dragged that into it."

"It's not just the show," Freddie said, tapping the timeline. "She noted real things. The church bell repair, the stoplight, and the man with the limp."

Pru's mouth quirked. "Sweetheart, you've only been here a few days and you've watched a lot of murder mystery television in your life AND you have a very active imagination, like your grandmother."

Freddie flinched; the gentleness of it stung more than if Pru had snapped. "I know how it sounds," she said. "But I saw him at the funeral. He shook my hand, then hid behind a gravestone and limped away when I looked back at him. And yesterday at the library, someone with the same gait was there when I was asking questions about the bell."

Pru sat back, teacup poised midair. "The library."

"And this." Freddie slid the threatening note closer with one fingertip. "Someone doesn't want me asking questions. Why, if there isn't anything to find?"

Pru didn't answer immediately. She set down her cup, reached for Winnie's map, and smoothed it with the heel of her hand. "Winifred's drawing skills were a crime in themselves," she said, but her smile was absent. Her gaze snagged on a scribble by the church and the wobbly arrow toward Main Street. "Left leg drags," she read softly. "Stutters under pressure."

Freddie waited.

Pru's jaw tightened, a small click of teeth behind the lips. "I don't like this," she said. "I don't like even saying it out loud." She drew a breath. "But, yes. I've seen him too. I'm not saying any of this else is true," she said with a wave of her hand over all of the papers, "But I saw him on occasion also." Then she folded her hands properly in her lap.

Freddie's chair creaked as she leaned forward. "When?"

Pru kept staring at the map, as if the answer might crawl out of the ink. "First time... well it was twenty or so years ago. I'd opened the bakery not too many years before that. He came in once or twice near closing. Kept to himself. Ordered coffee, didn't drink it. Stood in the corner like he was waiting for a bus that wasn't ever coming." She rubbed her forearm without seeming to notice. "He made me cold. Like standing in the shade too long on an autumn evening."

"The limp?"

"Same foot-dragging hitch." Pru hesitated. "And when Mrs. Halpern tried to chat him up about the weather, he...stumbled on his words. Not just shy, like his mouth couldn't catch his mind unless you pinned him in place."

Freddie felt the hairs lift on her own arms.

"And then?" she asked.

"Then nothing," Pru said. "He stopped coming in. People stopped mentioning him. Life does that." She swallowed. "Except...a few months ago, I thought I saw him again. Near the feed store, by the old Motor Court. He was across the street, and I told myself it was some man with a bad hip. I had a delivery to make and no time for ghosts. Also, it took me a little while to place that limp, but once you see it, it's hard to forget, you know."

Freddie reached for the list where Winnie had written **Sightings: twice outside bakery, once near church.** She underlined *bakery* and *church* with a shaking hand.

Pru blew out a breath, steady but thin. "I don't want to believe any of this means what you think it does. This is Fernridge, where we have pie committees and men who argue under the barber pole. We don't have—" She broke off, and when she spoke again, her voice was a whisper. "We don't have murder."

Freddie looked at the folder. At the note on the table. At the empty chair where Winnie should have been sitting, rolling her eyes and saying *of course we do, darling, it's just usually poorly plotted*.

"I didn't either," Freddie said. "Until I did."

Pru closed her eyes for a moment like she was bracing against a gust. When she opened them, something had shifted. Not belief, exactly. Permission to proceed.

"Alright," she said. "We're not going to repeat that 'M' word tonight, it's not officially a word I'm agreeing has happened here, in my town." She held up a hand before Freddie could argue. "But we *are* going to keep our eyes open. Quietly. I'll ask around without asking around. And you—" She tapped the note. "You don't go anywhere alone after dark. And if you get another note like that one, you tell me first."

Freddie nodded. Aggie, who had been pretending to nap, opened one eye and chirruped in what sounded like agreement.

They drank their tea in a momentary peace that felt made, not found. Freddie marked the timeline with the facts Pru had given her: **feed store, months ago; bakery, 20ish years; same limp; speech**

more normal when cornered. She wrote it neatly, the way she wrote everything, as if tidiness could keep fear from smudging the edges.

The front bell chimed.

All three of them looked up. Pru frowned and glanced at the *CLOSED* sign in the window. "I could have sworn I locked that door, but Kevin has a key," she said hesitantly. "Though he doesn't usually stop by without being asked."

Footsteps padded over worn floorboards. A familiar voice floated in, wry and careful and not belonging to Kevin. "Forgive the intrusion. I saw a light and assumed either hospitality or a séance."

Nigel Ashcroft stopped in the doorway, a benign picture in a navy blazer and a tie he might have tied twice. His gaze took in the mugs, the folder, the scattered pages—the way Freddie's hand moved, quick as a magician's, to pull a book across the worst of the mess.

"Evening," he said, soft as lamplight.

Pru was already half out of her chair, smile snapped into place. "How'd you get in? I know I locked that door."

Nigel shook his head. "It wasn't locked, knob just twisted right open." He shrugged like it was neither here nor there that he'd managed to waltz through a locked door.

"You missed the pie coup," Pru told him, changing the subject before Nigel began to wonder why they were so adamant about locking the door to a store that should be open. "Justice will never recover."

Nigel winced. "I was detained by an overly helpful gentleman who wished to recount, in real time, an episode from 2008." He smiled at Freddie. It didn't quite reach his eyes. "I came to see if you needed anything. Tea. Company. An entertaining story."

"We're alright," Freddie said, not moving her hand from the book. Her pulse had picked up for reasons that had nothing to do with fandom.

Nigel's gaze flicked, just once, to the edge of the red-circled words peeking from beneath the hardback: **A Murder Most Unsolved**. His expression didn't change, but something behind it did; a tightening, a settling, the way a man prepares to answer a question he hopes won't be asked.

He recovered with an elegant shrug. "Well then. I'll leave you to it." He turned to Pru. "If you should, by some miracle, have any cherry pie left, I would kill for a slice."

Pru swatted his arm with a dish towel. "Don't say *kill* in the kitchen."

He laughed, a little too high in the throat, and backed into the hall. "I'll mind my verbs."

When he'd gone, the silence he left behind wasn't empty; it was full of things unsaid.

Pru exhaled. "He's harmless," she said with the certainty of someone who believed it into being. "Nigel's a show pony. He couldn't hurt a moth."

Freddie stared at the book under her palm. "Maybe," she said.

Aggie flicked his tail against her wrist, as if reminding her that even show ponies can bite if you stick your hand in the wrong place.

Pru picked up the threatening note again and slid it back into her apron. "Tomorrow," she said, "we bake before we brainstorm. Brains go better with butter."

Freddie nodded. She gathered Winnie's papers into a stack and retied the ribbon. The knot felt firmer now. Not an ending. The start of something that would hold.

12

THE FERNRIDGE MOTOR COURT

By morning, the town had shaken off its poetry hangover and gone back to being Fernridge. The bakery windows fogged with sugar steam and the doorbell dinged every six seconds as customers came and went. Somewhere nearby a wind chime insisted on playing the same three notes like it had a vendetta.

Pru slid a pan of cinnamon braids from the oven and thumped it onto the counter between them. "Fuel," she declared. "Investigations run on butter."

Freddie took a bite and made a helpless sound that was ninety percent pastry and ten percent relief. Then she squared Winnie's folder on the table like a general unfurling a battle map.

"Motor Court," she said. "The women at the picnic said the limping man's renting near the feed store."

Pru wiped her hands on her apron, eyes narrowing with purpose. "Shoes. Sunglasses. Attitude that says 'we absolutely belong wherever we go.'"

"You always have that attitude," Freddie insisted.

"Fake it till you bake it."

A MURDER MOST UNSOLVED

They cut down Elder Lane past the shopfronts to where town frayed into parking lots and utility poles. The Fernridge Motor Court sat back from the road, a horseshoe of single-story rooms painted a hopeful pastel blue. A Coke machine hummed beside the office door; above it, a hand-lettered sign announced WEEKLY RATES / NO PARTIES / ICE IS FOR GUESTS NOT FISH.

Inside the office, the air conditioner rattled like a jar of buttons. A woman with cropped steel-gray hair and readers on a chain looked up from a crossword. She wore a navy polo with PENNY stitched over the pocket and the expression of someone who could set a broken bone with a tongue depressor and duct tape.

"Help you?" she asked.

"Penny Caldwell?" Pru leaned on the counter, a charm offensive in sunflower earrings. "We're from The Marple & Quill."

Penny's face softened by a millimeter. "Winnie's girls."

The words landed in Freddie's chest with a small, warm thud. She nodded. "I'm Freddie."

Penny patted the counter like she might pat a skittish horse. "I liked your grandmother," she said. "She brought me coffee here when my compressor quit in August and I was one degree from throwing this whole place into the river."

"We're trying to... tie up some loose ends," Freddie said. "Quietly."

Penny's eyes cut to the dusty window, then back. "Loose ends got a way of tying around your ankles if you don't mind 'em." She slid the crossword aside. "If you got loose ends, then you must be looking for the fella."

Freddie's throat tightened. "He stays here?"

Penny sniffed. "Stayed. On and off. Cash only. Keeps odd hours. Room Six when he's in. Signs 'E. Pike' on the pad, which isn't a name so much as a fishing plan."

"Left leg?" Pru asked softly, making an awkward gesture with her hand to simulate his off-balance walk.

"Drags like he's pulling a dock behind him." Penny tipped her chin toward the lot. "He checked out last night quick as a rabbit. No 'see you later.' No nothing."

"Could we…" Freddie glanced toward the row of rooms and then back, not quite able to finish the sentence.

Penny chewed on the inside of her cheek for a beat, then decided. "You can look from the doorway," she said. "I didn't flip it yet. Haven't had the…motivation yet."

She grabbed a jangling ring of keys and led them out into the sunlight. Room Six sat at the bend of the horseshoe, half-shaded by a scraggly crepe myrtle. Penny unlocked it and pushed the door open with two fingers like a magician unveiling a disappointing trick.

The room was the kind every roadside room becomes if no one loves it: plain bedspread, bolted lamp, a table with one good leg and one that has opinions. The air smelled faintly of cigarettes and cheap cleaner.

"Don't touch," Penny said, but gently.

Freddie stood at the threshold. Little things bloom when you look for them. A coffee ring ghosted on the windowsill. The flimsy plastic trash can, empty, liner gone. On the table, a church bulletin from last Sunday had been used as a coaster; a faint brown circle branded the upcoming events page.

Freddie's gaze snagged on the dresser. A magazine lay askew, *Southern Outdoorsman*, and peeking from beneath it, the torn corner of a

A MURDER MOST UNSOLVED

Fernridge Gazette. She crouched without crossing the line of the door and tilted her head to read.

Lightning Damages Church Bell

The headline was from 1998. Freddie didn't realize she'd stopped breathing until she heard herself start again.

Pru's hand hovered near her shoulder. "You see it?"

"He's not the first guest who kept old clippings," Penny said, watching their faces. "I had a woman keep three years of obits 'cause she said her cousin was bound to come through sooner or later." Her mouth twisted. "He never did."

"Any mail left for him?" Freddie asked, trying to think of anything that might help them figure out who he really was.

"Nah, he never got anything here. Maybe a box at the post office?" Penny said, giving one more lead to follow up on soon.

"Did anyone come looking for him?" Freddie asked. "Last night. This morning."

Penny considered. "A man in a navy blazer walked the lot around dusk. Didn't come in. I figured he was lost or had too many drinks down at the watering hole."

Freddie and Pru exchanged a glance.

"Navy blazer?" Pru whispered mostly to herself as the idea set in that it might have been Nigel. "British?"

Penny squinted, replaying. "Could've been. He had that…tidy way of walking. Like he irons his thoughts." She shrugged. "Didn't do anything. Just looked like a man who couldn't find his car. But I didn't get close enough to hear him speak."

Freddie's stomach did a small, slow seesaw. Red herring or major clue she wasn't sure, but she was tempted to pull that thread and find out. But she'd just note it for now and not tug...yet.

"Thank you," she said. "We won't take more of your time."

Penny relocked Room Six and pocketed the keys. "You be careful," she said pointe

dly and not as an afterthought. "I got the feeling off that fella like you get from a thunderhead, no rain yet, but your dog's already hiding under the bed."

On their way past the office, the Coke machine thunked to life like it wanted attention. As badly as Freddie could use a Diet Coke to stabilize her nerves, she wasn't sure the freshness of anything coming from this vending machine could be trusted, so she decided against it.

Freddie glanced down the motel row one last time. A shadow shifted at the far end, just beyond the laundry room, there, then gone. The angle, the light, the easy way emptiness throws tricks. Still, her skin tightened along her forearms.

"See something?" Pru asked, already looking in the direction Freddie was looking.

"Maybe." Freddie forced her feet to keep moving forward. "Let's go."

They thanked Penny again and stepped back into Fernridge's ordinary noise, the feed store bell, a lawn mower somewhere giving its all, cicadas sizzling the air.

By the time they reached The Marple & Quill, Freddie's adrenaline had worn down to a thin wire. Pru shooed her toward the counter. "Sit," she said. "I'll make tea and a grilled cheese the size of your face."

A MURDER MOST UNSOLVED

Aggie materialized from under a chair like a magician's prop and launched himself onto the counter, sprawling across the old-fashioned landline phone as if he'd personally invented telecommunications.

"You are not in tech support," Freddie told him, rubbing his chin. He rewarded her by turning himself into an even heavier loaf.

The shop was quiet. The kind of quiet that lets small sounds tap louder: kettle beginning to murmur, the click of the chalkboard marker as Pru fixed a crooked S, the tiny mechanical whir of the phone's answering machine as its digital light blinked from 0 to 1.

Freddie frowned. "Did we...get a call?"

Pru poked her head around the corner. "Kevin maybe. He keeps forgetting if we're out of nutmeg."

Aggie's tail thumped. His paw slid over the answering machine like a furry paperweight and hit PLAY.

A hiss of static. Then a breath. Then a voice: low, hoarse, close to the microphone.

"Stop." A swallow. "Stop...asking questions."

The words tripped slightly at the edge of asking, as if snagged on the speaker's tongue.

"For your own good," the voice said. The line clicked dead.

Pru was already at Freddie's side, towel in one hand, eyes fixed and stern in a way Freddie had never seen. "Well," she said, voice remarkably calm. "That's not neighborly."

Freddie rewound, listened again. Stop... asking. The catch wasn't much—but once you heard it, you couldn't unhear it.

"We call Lila?" Pru asked, meaning Deputy Barrett.

Freddie stared at the 1 lighting up the machine, then at Aggie's unruffled whiskers, then at Winnie's folder on the stool where she'd set it down. She felt the fear, acknowledged it, set it gently on a shelf inside her chest. Then she shook her head.

"Not yet," she said. "We're not ready, we don't know enough. For now, let's just write it down for our records and keep researching." She reached for a pen. "Time, message, every syllable."

Pru blew out a breath that sounded like a little bit of agreement with a lot of annoyance. "Fine. We document, we tea, we research but eventually we phone the law. We also bake triple-chocolate retaliation cookies because if someone's going to be rude, we will be rude right back with butter."

Aggie, satisfied that his role in today's part of the investigation had been fulfilled, flopped onto his side and began to purr, loud as a small engine.

Freddie wrote: **Voicemail—12:47 p.m.—male voice? hoarse. "Stop... asking questions. For your own good." Slight catch on 'asking.'**

She underlined the catch. Twice.

And for a moment, as the kettle sang and Pru clattered teacups like a general loading cannons, Freddie felt very much like she was exactly where she was supposed to be: in a bookstore, with a cat and a friend and a folder full of truth that didn't want to stay buried.

13

THE INTRUDER

All afternoon, the storm had been gathering its forces, stacking heavy clouds over Fernridge like someone slowly pulling a thick quilt across the sky. The air had that pre-rain tension to it, warm but restless, carrying the faint metallic scent of lightning waiting to strike. By the time Freddie flipped the CLOSED sign on The Marple & Quill's front door, the wind had a bite to it, and the green awning outside rattled like it might rip free at any second.

Pru had left an hour ago to finish up a special order at the bakery, promising to swing back with dinner. Freddie had smiled and waved her off, saying she'd be fine.

Inside, the shop felt smaller in the dimming light, every shadow sharper, every creak in the floorboards louder. She moved methodically, the way you do when you're alone in a big space and pretending you're not listening for footsteps that aren't there. She stacked stray books, slid chairs back under tables, and clicked off lamps one by one. Rain began to spit against the front windows in sporadic bursts, like impatient fingers drumming.

When she reached the rear section near the cookbooks, the power gave a sullen flicker. For half a breath, she stood in darkness, Aggie's bell-like collar jingling somewhere behind her. Then the lights stuttered back to life, casting everything in a yellow haze.

She took a steadying breath. She was jumpy because of the weather, she told herself. Not because of the strange message, or her own growing file of uneasy encounters in Fernridge, or the limping man whose face had started showing up in her dreams.

A sound like a muffled *scrape* came from the back alley.

She froze, heart thudding in her ears.

The crack of splitting wood followed.

She turned toward the noise just as the rear door banged inward, ricocheting off the wall. A figure in a hooded jacket slipped inside, moving fast and low. The smell of wet wool and cigarette smoke rushed in with them.

They didn't look at her; instead, they went straight for the cookbooks.

"Hey!" Freddie's voice came out louder than she knew possible, the word bouncing off the high ceiling. "What are you—"

The figure didn't answer. Books began hitting the floor in fast succession as gloved hands shoved them aside. Their movements weren't random, they were looking for something. Her stomach dropped.

Winnie's folder. Hidden behind *Southern Pies & Biscuit Dreams*.

"Don't you dare—" She took a step toward them, but the intruder spun, shoulder slamming into her hard enough to send her stumbling into a shelf. Pain bloomed through her entire body.

The manila edge of the folder flashed in the intruder's grip.

Aggie got there first.

With a yowl like a war trumpet, the cat launched himself off the counter in a furry blur, claws outstretched. He landed squarely on the intruder's arm, claws catching fabric, teeth snapping shut on the thick sleeve.

The folder slipped free and skidded across the floor.

"Get off!" The voice was loud, while its high-pitched tone reflected the panic; it didn't give away the person's gender. The intruder wrenched backward, tearing loose a patch of jacket that came away with a tuft of Aggie's fur. The fabric dangled for a second before dropping to the floor.

Then they bolted. Boots pounded the alley pavement, swallowed almost immediately by the wind and rain. The door slammed on its hinges, shuddering against the frame.

Freddie stood there, pulse hammering, Aggie hissing like he'd just repelled an invading army. She ran to the backdoor, bolting it shut before forcing her fingers to work her phone. "Lila? It's Freddie. You need to get here. Now."

Deputy Lila Barrett arrived in under five minutes, the storm plastering her dark ponytail to her jacket. Her boots left small puddles across the wood floor as she scanned the room with a sweep that was all cop, efficient, clinical, already assembling a picture.

"Tell me everything," she said, voice low but firm.

Freddie recounted the break-in, editing as she went. She left out the folder's significance, trying to make it sound like random vandalism. The Deputy didn't interrupt, but when Freddie finished, her eyes lingered on her just a fraction too long, like she was measuring the weight of what hadn't been said.

"Doorframe's split," Deputy Barrett said finally, crouching to examine it. "Handyman'll have to replace it, but for now just keep it bolted closed to keep the rain out. You hurt?"

"Just a bruise," Freddie said. "Aggie, on the other hand, should be given the key to the city."

The cat, now grooming his paw like nothing had happened, ignored them both.

Deputy Barrett used her pen to pick up the scrap of torn jacket. She dropped it into an evidence bag and held it up to the light. "Black fabric. And...long orange-colored fur?" She arched a brow toward Aggie.

"From the intruder," Freddie said jokingly. "Aggie's an orange tabby, not a coat donor."

The corner of the Deputy's mouth ticked upward. "Right. I'll keep it in evidence."

The bell over the front door jangled, letting in a rush of cold air and Nigel Ashcroft in a dripping trench coat. He froze in the doorway, eyes sweeping the shop before locking on the busted back door.

"Back door's damaged?" His voice was tight. "I heard it from down the block."

Freddie's head snapped up. "You... heard it?"

"Yes. A loud crack—wood giving way. I was at the theatre, and the alley runs right behind, well, I came straight here after I got dressed and locked up." He gestured vaguely, as though that settled it or should have meant anything to them.

She nodded slowly, but the image of him just happening to be within earshot while the break-in happened pricked at the back of her mind. Why would Nigel be locking up the theatre?

Nigel's gaze gave her a once-over. "Are you hurt?"

"I'm fine," she said, though her voice sounded sharper than she'd intended.

"This is ghastly," he said, stepping closer. "You can't stay here alone tonight. I'll—"

The front door swung open again cutting off Nigel, this time revealing Pru in a whirlwind of rain-slick hair and bakery warmth.

"Sweet butter biscuits, I leave you for two hours—" She stopped short, eyes darting between Freddie, Nigel, and Lila. "What happened?"

"She was nearly knocked flat," Nigel said before Freddie could answer. "I'll stay with her until the door's repaired."

"No, you won't," Pru said briskly, peeling off her wet jacket. "You'll get her upstairs with some tea while I see to the shop."

"I can lock up myself—" Freddie started.

Pru gave her the kind of look that could halt stampeding cattle. "Upstairs. Now."

Nigel offered his arm again. She hesitated, catching the Deputy's gaze over his shoulder. The deputy's expression was professional, but there was a flicker there—something that said *I'll be back tomorrow, and we're going to talk more.*

Freddie finally let Nigel lead her toward the secret bookshelf door, Aggie weaving between her legs like nothing at all had happened.

Still, the thought needled at her: how exactly had Nigel known about the break-in before even stepping inside?

And why had the intruder gone straight for Winnie's cookbooks? How did they know where things were hidden?

14

The Hollow Book

The morning after the break-in dawned reluctantly, dragging a slate-gray light through the front windows of The Marple & Quill. Rainwater streaked the glass in thin, uneven streams, and the smell of wet pavement seeped in each time a customer cracked the door. Fernridge was quieter than usual, as though the storm had wrung it out and left it damp and subdued.

Freddie had been up since six, not that it mattered because sleep had been more of an on-and-off negotiation than an actual rest. Every time she closed her eyes, she saw the shadowed figure in the cookbook section, the gloved hands shoving books aside, and the flash of manila in their grip. And Aggie's leap, a ridiculous, heroic, perfectly-timed leap, looped in her mind like the end of a sports highlight reel. Aggie truly was better than any top-notch guard dog.

She'd finally decided that the intruder must be watching her; how else would they have known where she hid Winnie's notes? She only just put them back in the cookbook section for safe keeping.

She'd decided the best way to steady her nerves was to do something normal. For her, that meant reshelving the chaos the break-in had left behind.

Aggie had other ideas.

"Not helpful," she murmured as the cat, her self-appointed supervisor, stretched himself luxuriously across an entire shelf in the nonfiction section. He had chosen the precise spot she was about to tidy, because of course he had.

She bent to lift him and froze.

Beneath his plump orange form was a single book, its black-and-crimson dust jacket standing out against the bland spines of gardening manuals and local history. *Murder at the Vicarage.*

The wrong place entirely. Winnie would never have allowed one of her beloved Christies to languish in nonfiction, let alone between *Composting Made Simple* and *A History of American Mills.*

"A little off your usual turf, Aggs," she said softly. Aggie yawned in response, as if to say *Exactly where I meant to be.*

She slid the book free. It felt...wrong. Lighter than it should be. And when she thumbed the pages, they didn't separate. Instead, they fanned stiffly around a rectangular cavity carved into the center.

Her chest tightened.

The hollow was neatly lined with yellowing tissue paper. Nestled inside were three things:

A small folded note in Winnie's unmistakable looping script.

A scrap of lined paper bearing a quick, rough pencil sketch of a figure standing with toes turned slightly out and the left shoulder dipped lower than the right.

A longer list, written in ballpoint and underlined twice:

Storm → Bell/stoplight → Missing man

Freddie set the book down on the nearest table and unfolded the first note.

Only five words, written in Winnie's hand but underlined as though she'd pressed the pen down hard: **He never left. Not really.**

She whispered the phrase under her breath, as though it might sound different aloud, make more sense when spoken. It didn't.

Her gaze shifted to the sketch. The stance was distinctive, and even in a quick drawing, the imbalance was obvious. She could almost see the hitch in the figure's gait. Aggie, still sprawled on the shelf, gave a low, questioning *mrrow*, as if he, too, recognized it.

Freddie's mind flicked back to the funeral. The way his step had seemed minor at first, then deepened to that odd dragging hitch when he moved away from her. Left leg drags. Stutters under pressure. Winnie's earlier notes matched.

And then there was the list.

The first item sent her mind straight back to her conversation with Father Keating a few days earlier. Summer of '98, a storm so fierce that lightning struck the church tower and destroyed the bell mechanism. That much he'd offered willingly. But when she'd asked if anyone had been injured during the repairs, the warmth had cooled from his voice, and he'd redirected the conversation so neatly she'd almost admired it. *Withholding, not suspect*, she'd decided at the time. But seeing storm and bell here, written in Winnie's decisive hand, made her sure the bell wasn't just for show. Something, or someone, important was connected to that storm.

And the missing man, this was new information but Freddie didn't need help there. That one lived in her chest like an old bruise. The town had believed her father left on his own. Winnie had clearly thought otherwise. Maybe this whole chain of clues was her way of proving it. Proving her son hadn't unceremoniously abandoned his family. The timeline fit too perfectly to not think all this might be related to her father's disappearance from Fernridge. Freddie just wasn't sure yet if that made him a victim or an accomplice.

She sat back in the chair, rubbing her forehead. Winnie's breadcrumbs always seemed straightforward until you took the first step, and then they slipped sideways. Still, there was something urgent here. **He never left** was not an observation. It was a warning.

A sharp rap on the front window broke her concentration. Penny Caldwell, the Motor Court manager, waved cheerfully before hustling past, her umbrella nearly inverting in the wind. Freddie waved back absently.

Her eyes returned to the hollow book. She couldn't leave this here, not with someone actively searching for Winnie's stash. The book and its contents went into her bag, Aggie following the motion like a tennis match.

"I know," she said. "It's getting harder to keep up, isn't it?"

Aggie blinked at her, which she took as agreement.

She thought through her next move. If Winnie had been chasing a real-life *Father Grey* mystery, it wasn't just because she loved the show. She'd recognized something, some overlap between a fictional crime and the people around her. And she'd baited Nigel into Fernridge with the promise of "industry connections."

That could only mean Rupert.

Rupert Whitcomb was Fernridge's grand old man of the stage, director of the community theatre for nearly half a century. He was ninety if he was a day, but he still wore silk scarves and insisted on being called "Maestro." Winnie had adored him, once; she'd even joked about putting his headshot in the window next to the new releases.

If Rupert had been her supposed connection for Nigel, he might know more about how the episode *A Murder Most Unsolved* came to be. Had Winnie told him about any of this or about Nigel's possible arrival in Fernridge?

Her mind made the decision before she could talk herself out of it: she'd go to the theatre. Talk to Rupert. Ask him directly.

By mid-morning, the rain had shifted to a drizzle, making the streets appear gloomy and reflective. Customers trickled in, shaking off umbrellas, pausing to chat about the storm damage, mostly branches down, and one unfortunate chicken coop collapse on the east side, but thankfully, no chickens were injured. Freddie went through the motions: ringing up paperbacks, making small talk, feeding Aggie his midday treat. She was getting good at this running-a-bookstore thing, she thought as she smiled to herself.

But her thoughts still kept going back to the hollow book in her bag.

Around two, Pru came in with a basket of warm cheddar-chive biscuits and an armful of gossip about the locals. She set them down with a flourish. "Eat two of these and you'll forget you were almost brained by a burglar," she said.

Freddie smiled, but her mind was still in the back of the shop. "Pru... can you cover the counter for an hour? I need to run an errand."

"Errand, or snooping?" Pru asked, narrowing her eyes in mock suspicion.

"Both," Freddie admitted.

Pru grinned. "You're finally speaking my language. Let's lock up, and I'll come with."

They left The Marple & Quill, Freddie with her coat buttoned tight and her bag containing all of Winnie's notes pressed to her side. She wasn't naïve enough to think whoever had broken in wouldn't try again. And until she figured out what Winnie had been chasing, and why, it was safer to keep the clues close.

As she passed the church, she slowed. The bell tower loomed against the pale sky, its cross silhouetted like an exclamation point. She thought of Father Keating's careful smile, his smooth redirection, and the way his fingers had lingered on his cuff buttons before answering her. There was more there. Something she'd have to pull loose.

But not today.

Today, she turned toward the theatre district, the single block of Fernridge that dared to call itself that, and felt the first stirrings of real promise and purpose in days. The fear was still there, sure, but it had an edge of determination now.

Winnie had left her clues.

And Freddie was finally ready to follow them.

15

CATS AND CUPS AND CORPSES, OH MY

The Fernridge Community Theatre sat like an old footstool someone couldn't bear to throw away; scuffed at the corners, threadbare in places, but still sturdy where it mattered. A squat brick box with a marquee too small for its dreams, it huddled between a shuttered antiques store and a pizza place that smelled perpetually of oregano and hope. Hand-cut letters on the sign announced:

COMING SOON — AND THEN THERE WERE NONE

Someone had carefully centered the dash and then had given up on centering anything else.

Freddie pushed the door open and stepped into the dim lobby. The floor creaked, and the scent of paint and sawdust hit her nose. A long folding table was set up with a stack of freshly copied programs, and two older women sat behind it, folding them neatly in half.

Both looked up at once.

"Well, bless my soul, it's Winifred March's girl," one of them exclaimed, squinting over her glasses. She had a neat crown of white curls and a brooch shaped like a violin pinned to her sweater. "The likeness is uncanny."

Freddie managed a small smile. She'd been in Fernridge barely a week, but half the town seemed to recognize her by sight. "Yes, ma'am. Freddie March."

The other woman sniffed, holding up a program. "They've gone and printed *refreshments at intermission,* but we all know Prudence never makes enough lemon bars. Gone by curtain every year."

"I heard that!" Pru called cheerfully from behind Freddie. "I'll double the batch this time, maybe triple if Rupert eats his usual amount."

The first woman chuckled, while the second pursed her lips as though reserving judgment until opening night.

Another man, leaning on a mop in the corner, muttered, "Triple won't help if Ed sneaks in early like he always does." He winked at Freddie. "This town eats faster than it applauds."

Freddie excused herself politely and followed Pru deeper into the building.

The lobby gave way to the auditorium, a wide hall with mismatched seating—some velvet, some folding chairs, and a stage at the far end. There, amid paint cans and precarious ladders, Rupert Whitcomb stood like a maestro at the center of chaos.

He wore a paisley silk scarf thrown dramatically over one shoulder and held a tiny hammer in his hand like it was a conductor's baton.

"No, no, no! The staircase must creak here, not there! What good is *And Then There Were None* if the stairs don't groan like death's door?"

"Rupert," Pru said, sweeping in with a mock curtsey. "Your audience has arrived."

Rupert turned, spotted them, and his face broke into an expression of pure delight. "Winifred's granddaughter!"

He hurried down the steps, moving faster than seemed advisable for a man of his age. "Oh, how she adored this place. Donated half our props closet, you know. Told me once I made this place feel legitimate." His eyes grew watery, but he smiled fiercely. "And legitimate we remain."

Freddie felt her throat tighten. "She talked about you often in her letters. Said you could make even plywood look dignified."

"Plywood *is* dignified if you treat it with respect," Rupert declared, then immediately shouted up at the stage crew, "Not like that! Mind the nails, darling, or the leading lady will impale herself before act two, and she doesn't die till the final act."

On stage, a man in overalls threw his hands up. "It's a *volunteer* crew, Rupert. No one signed a waiver for mortal peril."

A ripple of laughter went through the theatre. Even the boy sweeping the aisle nearby, an usher trainee barely fourteen, snorted. He gave Freddie a conspiratorial glance, then deadpanned toward an incoming person over her shoulder: "Want me to get the first-aid kit again, Mr. Ashcroft?"

Nigel, who had appeared as if conjured, clutched his chest in mock offense. "Young man, my dignity is intact, thank you."

The teen smirked. Pru burst out laughing, and Rupert waved a distracted hand. "Carry on, carry on."

Aggie, who had followed Freddie in despite the drizzle, chose that moment to leap onto the stage. Freddie still hadn't figured out how Aggie managed to get out of the bookstore whenever he felt like galivanting around town, but she was convinced he could either open doors on his own or that there was a hidden cat door that led outdoors that she wasn't aware of. Aggie sniffed at a pile of fabric, then triumphantly dragged out a lace doily from a basket of props. Tail held high, he paraded across the boards like a catwalk model.

"Marvelous creature," Rupert announced. "He has stage presence. Keep him."

Nigel crouched dramatically as though preparing to wrestle the doily away, but Aggie evaded him with feline grace, hopping down into the orchestra pit to continue his parade.

"Someone catch that cat!" a voice called from the wings.

"No, just let him!" Rupert countered. "It adds verisimilitude. *Chaos is character!* Plus, you'll never catch that ornery creature."

Freddie shook her head. Between Rupert's theatrics, Nigel's vanity, and Aggie's mischief, she wasn't sure who was winning the performance. But beneath the absurdity, she could sense why Winnie had loved this place; it was alive with energy, ridiculous and real all at once.

Rupert beckoned them closer to the side of the stage, lowering his voice. "Winifred had a nose for stories. She brought me a tall tale once. Something she was writing or trying to figure out or heard about, I don't recall exactly. She found out about it in a strange, roundabout way. It spoke of a death with tea, a book, and a bell that struck the wrong note. She said it reminded her of *Father Grey*."

Freddie's pulse quickened. A death with tea. A book. A bell. The words slotted too neatly into Winnie's hidden notes.

"Do you have anything she wrote down about it?" she asked.

Rupert shook his head. "No, no, she just told me about it. Said she wanted to think on it. But she told me it was one of those things that made the world tilt just a little, the way only mysteries do."

Freddie tucked the phrase away. The world tilting. She knew precisely what Winnie had meant.

One of the ladies from the lobby shuffled in with a box of costumes, overhearing. "Winnie always was poking around where she shouldn't. Remember when she insisted the ghost light flickered because of sabotage?"

Rupert chuckled fondly. "She was wrong, of course. It was just faulty wiring. But she made me *believe* for an evening, and isn't that theatre's whole purpose?"

Everyone within earshot nodded. A man painting a flat leaned over to his partner. "Didn't she also say that broken prop sword was connected to some feud at City Hall?"

"She *proved* it!" his partner whispered back, eyes gleaming. "It was borrowed during a budget disagreement. Winnie had the minutes to prove it."

Freddie smiled faintly, soaking in these bits of her grandmother's legend. Winnie hadn't just loved mysteries; she had woven them into Fernridge's daily life.

Before she could press further, Nigel clapped his hands, drawing all eyes back to him. "Well, since the truth is creeping toward the footlights, I might as well confess my part in it."

He leaned against a ladder, adopting the tone of a tragic hero. "The infamous *Murder Most Unsolved*, my crowning contribution to *Father Grey*, was not my original invention. It was based on a letter. An anonymous fan sent it years ago."

Nigel spread his hands. "I lost the envelope, alas, but I recall the postmark. Somewhere around here. Local, you see. I always suspected it was based on a real story, but, well, actors are given scripts, not evidence."

The usher teen snorted softly. "Translation: he can't keep track of his mail."

Pru elbowed him.

Freddie's suspicion flared. Convenient, wasn't it? An anonymous letter, an episode with eerie echoes of Winnie's notes and her death, and now Nigel just happened to remember the postmark? She studied his face, but his expression was a perfect mask of self-pitying sincerity.

"That sounds..." she began carefully, "awfully slippery."

Nigel winced, placing a hand over his heart. "Slippery? My dear, I am wounded."

But Rupert, watching with an unusual sharpness, muttered, "You remembered the phrase *bell struck wrong* before I even said it."

A ripple of silence. Nigel's eyes flicked, then smoothed over. "Perhaps I merely absorbed it."

Freddie filed the moment away. He had given himself away, if only slightly.

Pru rolled her eyes and cut in, "Oh, give him a break, Freddie. Nigel's not capable of keeping a secret, let alone committing a murder. The man narrates everything his mind thinks."

Nigel brightened instantly. "I do have a certain transparency."

Freddie wasn't so sure. His performance was good, maybe too good.

Before she could push him further, the back door banged open and a woman bustled in carrying a box of mismatched teacups. "Donations!" she called. "One of these belonged to my cousin, who swore someone was poisoned with it back in the '90s."

Rupert rolled his eyes skyward. "Thank you, Maureen. We'll add it to the arsenal."

Freddie, however, caught the way Pru's eyebrows shot up. Tea, again. Poison. Coincidence—or not?

Aggie leapt onto the box immediately, knocking a chipped cup onto its side and batting it like prey. He skittered off with it, leading half the crew in a comic chase up the aisle.

Rupert pressed his fingers to his temples. "Cats and cups and corpses, oh my. This play may yet kill me."

Laughter rippled across the stage crew, but Freddie barely heard it. She was still staring at Nigel, her mind whirring. A fan letter, local. A bell. A book. Tea. Winnie had followed the trail all the way here. And Freddie was beginning to see where it pointed.

As the rehearsal chatter swelled, Nigel adjusted his scarf and leaned close enough for only Freddie to hear. His smile was polished, but his voice carried an edge.

"You know, Miss March, sometimes chasing shadows only leaves you in the dark."

Freddie's breath caught.

He straightened instantly, voice booming again for the room. "Now then! Who will fetch me a proper cup of tea before Rupert insists we rehearse in silence?"

The others laughed, but Freddie's suspicion hardened. Nigel wasn't just a washed-up actor. He was holding something back.

Why was he even still in Fernridge?

16

THE POST OFFICE BOX

The Fernridge Post Office was hardly bigger than a convenience store, a squat brick building with peeling blue shutters and a faded mural of magnolia blossoms painted across one wall. Inside, it smelled faintly of paper, ink, and the burnt leftovers of yesterday's coffee. A row of brass P.O. boxes lined one wall like little bank vaults, their tiny keyholes glinting in the fluorescent light.

Pru leaned on the counter, tapping her nails against the glass. "Do you think they even deliver anything besides seed catalogs and utility bills anymore?"

"Depends on your definition of mail," Freddie said. She tried to sound casual, though her chest buzzed with nervous energy. Winnie's note had been clear: follow the trail. And the trail led here.

Behind the counter sat Mrs. Janice Henshaw, according to the large display nameplate, a woman whose hair had been set into the same immovable helmet for as long as anyone could remember. Her glasses perched on the end of her nose, and a crocheted tissue-box cover sat proudly beside the register like a guardian.

"Well, if it isn't Winifred's granddaughter," she said as they approached, voice carrying the brisk cheer of someone who had worked the same job for forty years and wasn't about to retire. "You've got her eyes, dear. She used to come in every Thursday for stamps, even when nobody writes letters anymore."

"She wrote me plenty," Freddie said softly.

"Course she did," Janice replied, as though confirming something she had long suspected. She snapped her gum, then leaned forward. "What can I do for you?"

Freddie exchanged a glance with Pru before saying, "I'm looking into some old P.O. box rentals. Around last year. Do you remember anyone paying cash, maybe under the name Pike?"

Janice pursed her lips. "Pike, Pike... We had a fella, yes. Didn't like paperwork, if you know what I mean. Wanted to keep it simple. Paid cash for six months at a time. Back then we didn't require ID, but that policy's changed since."

"Do you remember his first name?" Freddie asked.

"Just the initial." She tapped the counter for emphasis. "E. Pike. Tall fella. Wore a cap low. Not much of a talker. Gave me the willies, truth be told."

"That's him," muttered Pru.

"Box is closed now," Janice added. "He stopped paying months ago. We emptied it and sent what was left back to sender. Rules are rules."

Freddie felt her pulse quicken. A name, even a fragment but the same as the Motor Court. *E. Pike.* Though Penny had believed it was a fake name, it was still a connection.

Janice squinted at her. "Why you asking, dear? This about your grandma's stories? She was in here, nosing about that box once."

Freddie nodded. "Something like that."

Janice's voice softened. "Well, you be careful. Some boxes stay locked for a reason."

They'd just stepped out of the post office, the brass of the P.O. boxes still glinting in Freddie's mind, when a familiar cruiser eased to the curb. Deputy Barrett stepped out, adjusting her hat against the afternoon sun.

Her expression, when she spotted them, was not exactly welcoming. "March. Prudence." Her voice was cool but not unkind, the kind of tone that said she was balancing professionalism with a personal warning. "Funny seeing you two together, looking like you've got somewhere to be."

Freddie forced a smile. "Just heading to the library."

Barrett's eyes narrowed. "The library. Wouldn't have anything to do with...oh, say, poking around in matters you shouldn't be?" She rested one hand on her belt, not quite at her holster but close enough to remind them of her authority. "I'm still looking into your grandmother's death. And I don't need amateurs trampling through evidence, stirring up gossip, or making my job harder."

Pru shifted uneasily, and Freddie caught the way her friend's lips parted, ready to spill. Freddie cut her off quickly. "We're not interfering. Honestly. We're just looking into the history of some of Fernridge's monuments. They were Winnie's favorites, and we thought, well, it seemed like a way to feel close to her."

That, at least, was technically true. They were headed for the library, and Winnie had always loved the town's quirks.

Deputy Barrett studied her for a long moment, as if weighing the story against the stubborn glint in Freddie's eyes. Finally, she gave a curt nod. "Fine. But remember that there's a line between honoring someone and obstructing an investigation. Stay on the right side of it."

With that, she slid back into her cruiser, the engine rumbling as she pulled away from the curb.

Pru turned immediately, her voice low and urgent. "Freddie, we should have told her. About the box, about Pike. She's the law, for heaven's sake!"

"I know," Freddie said. She kept her gaze on the receding taillights, her grip tightening on her satchel. "But I can't. Not yet. Something about this feels bigger than we realize. If we hand it all over now, it'll get buried. I owe Winnie more than that."

Pru hesitated, torn, but finally sighed. "You're impossible, you know. Just like your grandmother."

"Maybe," Freddie said, forcing her feet to start moving again toward the library. "But impossible's the only way I know how to be right now."

The Fernridge Library, while not the grandest of locations, still had the perfect smell of old books and dreams. Afternoon sun spilled across oak tables, and the faint tick of the grandfather clock echoed down the aisles. Freddie carried a stack of city council minutes to a corner table where Pru had already set up camp with a soda and a pile of lemon drops. Aggie snuck into the library behind them and currently hid from the librarian under Pru's chair, curled into a little ball, ready to nap.

"Find anything scandalous yet?" Pru asked, popping candy into her mouth, research really wasn't her cup of tea, so she was currently offering assistance in the form of moral support.

"Depends on your definition of scandal," Freddie muttered, flipping through the bound volume from 1998. Her eyes skimmed the lines: motions carried, budgets approved, and permits issued. Then she stopped. "Here."

Council Meeting, July 7, 1998: *Emergency funding allocated to expedite installation of traffic light at Main & Elder. Contractor bids accepted from third-party subcontractors. Same contractor as current bell tower repairs at St. Mary's Catholic Church.*

Freddie frowned. "That's too neat. Both projects rushed through and taking place at the same time. And this subcontractor—'Southern Heritage Restorations.' Ever heard of them?"

Pru shook her head. "Sounds like someone naming companies out of a hat."

Freddie scanned further. "They don't appear again after that year. It's like they existed only to get those contracts."

"Shell company," Pru said with a shrug. "Half the town probably knew and looked the other way. Fernridge isn't famous for transparency. Not sure any small town is really."

Before Freddie could respond, an older man shuffled by their table, leaning on a cane. He peered down at the stack of papers. "Council minutes, eh? My wife reads those when she can't sleep. Works faster than warm milk."

Pru grinned. "Maybe we should donate them to Rupert for stage props. *The Boring Papers of 1998.*"

The man chuckled and shuffled off, leaving Freddie bent over the pages, her pen scribbling notes in the margin of her journal. *Bell repairs. Stoplight. Same week. Same contractors.*

By late afternoon, Freddie had moved on to an old stack of newspapers and clippings, the kind that made her eyes cross. She rubbed her temples, flipping pages until a headline snagged her attention:

Unidentified Worker Injured on Site

Her heart stuttered. She leaned closer.

The Fernridge Gazette, August 1998: *An unidentified construction worker was treated for a fractured ankle yesterday after an accident at a downtown site. The man declined to give his name and left before completing paperwork. Officials confirmed he was not a resident.*

"That's him," Freddie whispered.

"Who?" Pru perked up from her semi-unconscious state.

"The limping man," Freddie said. Her mind pieced it together: bell tower repairs, a fractured ankle, no name given. The man had been hiding even then.

Pru chewed her lip. "Could just be a coincidence. People twist ankles all the time."

"Not like this," Freddie said. She closed her eyes, picturing the limp, the way the man had dragged his leg. It fit perfectly.

By the time the library closed, the weight of the day pressed down on Freddie's shoulders. She and Pru walked back through the dusk, Aggie padding behind them with his tail held like a flag. The air smelled of rain-soaked earth and the distant tang of barbecue drifting from someone's backyard.

The bookstore sat quiet, its windows reflecting the glow of the streetlamps. Freddie bent to unlock the door when she noticed it: a white envelope slid halfway beneath the frame.

Her breath caught. She crouched and pulled it free. The paper was thick, yellowed slightly with age. Inside was a single torn page from the *Fernridge Gazette*. The headline leapt at her like a blow:

Daniel March Believed to Have Left Town

The article beneath was short, dismissive. *No search organized. But if anyone has heard from him recently, contact the Fernridge Police Department.*

Scrawled across the margin in block letters were four words:

LET IT STAY BURIED.

Freddie's throat closed. Her father's name. The town had decided he'd walked away. But Winnie hadn't believed it. And now neither did she.

Aggie pressed against her ankle, then darted forward to paw at the door. The envelope had dropped a few inches from his nose, and he stretched a paw beneath the frame as though trying to reach whoever had delivered it. His whiskers quivered, eyes wide, tail thrashing.

Pru knelt beside him, her voice low. "He smells something."

Freddie stared into the dark street beyond, but it was empty. Only the shadows stirred. Whoever had left the envelope was either gone or still out there, watching from somewhere she couldn't see.

She tightened her grip on the paper, her heart pounding. The trail wasn't just cold history anymore. Someone alive, here and now, wanted her to stop digging.

And, now, they were invoking her father's name to do it.

17

THE LIMPER'S TRAIL

Freddie told Pru she was going to bed early after a full day of working at The Marple & Quill.

It wasn't a complete lie. She did slip upstairs, change into her softest old T-shirt, and sit on the edge of the bed. But once the lights in the bookstore went out and Pru's footsteps faded away down the street toward her bakery flat, Freddie stayed wide awake.

Her heart thudded, and she knew it was the reckless abandon with which she was currently living her life, but it was a new feeling for her. She wasn't good at driving, wasn't good at improvising, but she was becoming very good at digging. And everything in her gut told her that Room 6 at the Fernridge Motor Court was a file cabinet drawer waiting to be opened.

The problem was, Pru no longer wanted to open it with her.

That afternoon Pru had grown sharp, sharper than Freddie had ever seen her. *"If we keep sniffing around like this, Barrett is going to think we're tampering with evidence. Or worse. I like a bit of drama, but this isn't Clue anymore, Freddie. This is dangerous. Someone is threatening you, Winnie just wouldn't stand for me letting you put yourself in danger, especially not for her."*

Freddie had nodded, promised to "let it rest for a night." And now here she was, lacing her sneakers tight and whispering to the empty shop: "I'm sorry, Pru. Just one more breadcrumb."

The Fernridge Motor Court looked even more unimpressive in the moonlight. A single buzzing streetlamp illuminated the gravel drive, accentuating the peeling mint-green paint and overgrown shrubbery. Freddie parked two blocks away and walked, her notebook heavy in her tote bag, her nerves heavier still.

She wouldn't have known to come here if not for Penny. The motel clerk had leaned over the counter earlier that morning, her voice dropping to a conspiratorial whisper.

"Room Six. Occupied again. Cash on the counter, name written sloppily—Pike. E. Pike. Same as before. Never lingers in the lobby, just takes the key and goes."

Penny tapped her temple knowingly. "Back of my mind always said trouble follows that one. Thought you should know, seeing as you're Winnie's girl."

Freddie had thanked her with as much calm as she could manage, but her palms had been sweaty ever since.

Now she stood in front of the door marked with a crooked brass 6. The window was dark, the curtain drawn. She reached for the knob, pulse racing. Locked. Of course. But when she shifted her weight, she saw it: the window slightly hanging open, someone had left in such a hurry they hadn't closed the it all the way.

Her throat tightened. Whoever "E. Pike" was, they were sloppy. Or maybe they wanted someone like her to find what they'd left behind. She guessed the latter, however.

She swallowed hard, slid the window open, and climbed in.

The smell hit first: damp carpet, old cigarettes, and something faintly medicinal. The bedside lamp buzzed when she turned it on, throwing weak light across a room that looked barely disturbed. She moved to pull the curtain completely closed so no one caught sight of the light's glare.

On the nightstand lay a folded clipping from the *Fernridge Gazette*. Freddie's hand shook as she unfolded it.

MARCH FAMILY ASKS FOR ASSISTANCE: Daniel March is currently missing, thought by some to have left town under suspicious circumstances. If you've heard from Mr. March, please contact the Fernridge police department or Winifred March.

Her father. Similar to the clipping left on her doorstep last night, only this one appeared to be published in the paper at a later time. Seeing it in this room, in someone else's possession, made her stomach clench. It was from months after he supposedly left town. Winnie hadn't believed the story everyone else did and eventually tried looking for him.

She laid it flat and forced herself to keep looking even though her emotions were all over the place.

On the desk, in an open box worn down at the edges: a hand-drawn sketch of the church tower, the lines heavy and uneven. The belfry ladder had been circled again and again until the paper nearly tore.

Next, tucked under the sketch, a brittle sheet of carbon paper. She held it up, heart hammering. Faint typewriter letters showed through:

It begins with an empty house and an old recluse, found with tea in his hand and a book by his side—

Margin notes crowded the edge in a shaky hand. *Not right. Not yet. Bell is key.*

Freddie's breath came fast. This wasn't just memorabilia. It was obsession. E. Pike was tracking her father, the bell, even Nigel's episode. The pieces were all tangled together, and she was standing in the knot.

The sound of crunching gravel outside froze her.

She doused the lamp instantly, heart in her throat. Through the curtain's crack, she saw wet footprints glistening under the streetlamp, stopping at the door. The shape outside shifted. For one breathless second, she thought the knob would turn.

Instead, silence. Then the scrape of shoes retreating, a limping rhythm, toe-out, uneven. The limp.

Freddie pressed a hand to her mouth. She didn't move until the footsteps faded entirely.

When she finally dared, she opened the window to leave the exact way she'd come, making sure to leave it cracked slightly as she'd found it. Rain had started, dampening the gravel, and the footprints shone brighter than the ground. She followed them across the parking lot to the edge of the Motor Court, where they ended abruptly at a storm drain. Water sloshed into the grate, carrying away any trace of further footprints.

She crouched, staring into the darkness down the road, shivering not from the rain but from the realization: he had been right here.

Watching. He knew someone was in his room. A shiver shook her body from both fear and the cool rain.

"Enjoying your evening stroll, Miss March?"

Freddie nearly leapt out of her sneakers. She jumped and spun around.

Deputy Barrett leaned against her cruiser in the motel lot, arms folded, one boot tapping. The cruiser's headlights were off, but the red-blue dash reflection painted her face in a way that made her look both weary and amused.

"I—" Freddie started, too fast. "I was just—"

Barrett's brow rose. "Investigating?"

The word cut sharper than the rain. Freddie tightened her grip on her tote bag. "No. I'm...I'm not investigating anything. Just out for air."

"Out for air at the Motor Court?" Barrett asked dryly. "Funny coincidence. I've had my eye on this place for weeks. And now I find you crawling out of a window?"

Freddie's stomach twisted. "I wasn't crawling—"

Barrett's gaze softened, but only slightly. "Look, I know you want answers about your grandmother. I get it. But you barging around like this, you could spook someone. You could wreck my case. Or even worse, you're gonna get yourself hurt if you aren't careful. Poke around the wrong place too hard and you'll get your finger bitten off."

Freddie swallowed hard, she was definitely afraid of that happening also.

"Your case?" she questioned the deputy.

"Yes, I'm still looking into your grandmother's death," Barrett said firmly. "You think I'm ignoring it, but I'm not. There are threads here, and I'm pulling them. The best thing you can do is not tangle the yarn."

Freddie's chest ached. She wanted to blurt out everything—the clipping, the sketch, the carbon sheet. Pru would have. But the words caught in her throat. She remembered how Pru's voice had nearly betrayed her earlier that week, how she'd almost confessed to Barrett about the bell and the limp.

Not yet. Not until she understood the shape of this puzzle. The deputy might stop at Winnie's killer, might solve that one piece of the puzzle, and then "Case Closed." But Freddie needed more answers than just that; she wasn't sure she could live without knowing everything.

She forced a smile that didn't feel right on her face. "I'm not interfering, Deputy. Honestly. I'm just...looking into some of the monuments around town. Winnie loved them, and I guess I just wanted to know more."

Barrett studied her, eyes narrowing, like she could see straight through the lie. Then she sighed. "Be careful, Freddie. Curiosity is a good quality until it isn't. And if you find yourself in over your head, call me." Her face softened. "Please don't play detective. I don't want you to get hurt, and I'm afraid that's exactly where this train is headed. Either that or I'll catch you crawling out of a window on private property again and arrest you," she said, finger wagging this one last warning directly in her face.

Freddie nodded, fingers crossed behind her back like a petulant child—after all, that's about how she was behaving.

Barrett shook her head, muttered something about "stubborn March women," and slid into her cruiser. The engine turned over, headlights flooding the lot before she pulled away.

Freddie exhaled only when the taillights vanished.

By the time she slipped back into The Marple & Quill, the rain had soaked her hair flat and her sneakers squelched on the wood floor. She leaned against the counter, shaking.

Aggie padded out of the shadows, tail swishing, and immediately began sniffing at her shoes. His whiskers twitched, and he sneezed twice before looking up at her accusingly.

"Motor oil," Freddie whispered, crouching to scratch his head. "From the drain. You smell it, don't you?"

He meowed and headbutted her hand, then went back to pawing her laces like he'd dig the truth out himself.

Freddie sat down hard on the rug, clutching her tote bag. Inside were the clipping, the sketch, the carbon sheet. Proof that someone, maybe the limper, was weaving her father, Winnie, Nigel, and the church bell into a single story.

She thought of Barrett's warning. She thought of Pru's frustration. But more than anything, she thought of Winnie.

"I can't stop now," she whispered into the dim shop. "Not until I know why."

Aggie purred, curling up against her side as if to anchor her to the floor. And for the first time that night, Freddie let herself cry, not out of fear, well, not only, but out of the raw certainty that she was getting closer. Too close, maybe.

The front bolt clicked.

"Freddie?" Pru's voice came softly through the dark. "You still up, sweetheart?"

Freddie swiped at her face with the back of her sleeve and stood, trying to look like a person who had definitely not climbed through a motel window. Pru stepped into the spill of light from the stairwell with a thermos and a towel over her arm.

"You left the lamp on upstairs," Pru said, eyes narrowing at Freddie's soaked hair and squelching shoes. "And you look like the rain chewed you up and spit you back out. Sit." She pressed the towel into Freddie's hands and set the thermos on the counter. "Chicken soup. Kevin's cure-all. Don't argue."

"I'm fine," Freddie said, the lie bitter on her tongue.

"I don't like the way your face looks when you say 'I'm fine,'" Pru replied, matter-of-fact. She leaned on the counter, studying her. "And I don't like secrets. Not the kind that might get people hurt."

Freddie's throat tightened. "I'm careful."

Pru's mouth tugged. "You're brave. Different thing entirely." She hesitated, then added lightly, "If you're going to run off alone, at least leave a note stuck to Aggie. He's the only one who'll tell me the truth."

Aggie, who had installed himself between them like a plush referee, chirped and pawed at Freddie's shoelace again, nose wrinkling at the oily scent.

Pru exhaled and backed toward the hall. "I'm not your warden, baby. I'm your people. Remember that. Lock the door behind me. And if Deputy Barrett shows up asking questions, tell her you were alphabetizing Agatha by adjective."

"Pru—" Freddie started.

Pru lifted a hand. "Tomorrow. Sleep first." She softened. "And Freddie? You don't have to carry her ghost alone. This town knows how to bury things, so you just watch yourself. I thought Kal leaving me behind was the biggest secret on Main Street, but you're proving me wrong."

When the door clicked shut, the shop felt larger and lonelier all at once. Freddie locked it, killed the front lamp, and slipped upstairs with her tote hugging her side.

In the apartment's hush, she unzipped the old floral couch cushion, the one with a tiny hidden seam she remembered from childhood, a spot where Winnie slipped love notes and stray crossword clues. She slid the three finds inside: the Gazette clipping about Daniel March, the tower sketch with the circled ladder, the brittle carbon with its shaky margin scrawl. She smoothed the fabric, set the cushion back, and watched as Aggie hopped up and kneaded it into a vigilant throne.

"Guard duty," she whispered. Aggie blinked solemnly: obviously.

Freddie stood a long moment by the lace-draped window, watching rain stitch silver diagonals across Main Street. She could still feel Deputy Barrett's stare like a hand on her shoulder; she could still hear Pru's quiet promise; I'm your people. The guilt pressed, but the need pressed harder.

"Soon," she told the dark. "I'll tell soon."

She clicked off the lamp. In the dim, the grandfather clock breathed its steady tick, the store below settled into its nighttime bones, and Freddie tucked herself beneath the afghan like an oath.

"Hold the line, Winnie," she whispered to the ceiling. "I'm not stopping."

18

THE STAGE IS SET

The Fernridge Community Theatre had never looked so alive. The rickety building hummed with so much energy that the brickwork was in fear of falling. This kind of excitement only came on the cusp of opening night. Posters for *And Then There Were None* were taped crookedly along the lobby walls, their edges curling in the humid summer air.

Inside the auditorium, the house lights glowed over a ragtag collection of mismatched seats. Velvet-covered rows from a defunct opera house sat side by side with metal folding chairs borrowed from the VFW. The scent of sawdust and fresh paint still clung to everything.

Freddie slid into a chair lining the stage beside Rupert, who wore a paisley scarf and carried a clipboard he clearly believed was his scepter. He leaned toward her, his voice was a stage-whispered but still carried easily.

"We've dedicated this performance to your grandmother," he said, eyes glistening. "The program reads: *For Winifred March, who knew every story deserves a stage.* She gave us props, donations, encouragement—most of all, legitimacy."

Freddie's throat tightened. She nodded, staring up at the stage where the painted backdrop of a gloomy island house was still drying. Winnie would have adored it, even with the brushstrokes uneven and the staircase wobbling underfoot.

Pru bustled past, balancing two trays of concessions, her apron dusted with powdered sugar. "Triple batch of lemon bars this time," she announced, "and if anyone complains they're gone by intermission, I'll make them eat Nigel's shortbread instead."

"I heard that," Nigel said smoothly from the wings. He stepped out in costume, an old three-piece suit pressed within an inch of its life, and tipped an imaginary hat. "Though I suppose the role calls for a touch of austerity. Consider me a sacrifice to Agatha Christie."

Rupert flapped his hands like a conductor. "Places, everyone! Remember, this is not merely a rehearsal, it is a memorial, a resurrection, a triumph!"

The bustle onstage intensified: teenagers in ill-fitting blazers carried flats, an older woman fussed with the hem of a dress with her mouth full of pins, and someone's little girl toddled down the aisle clutching a feather boa. Freddie felt the ache in her chest ease. For all its chaos, this was Fernridge alive, communal, messy, and devoted. And she was beginning to love it.

An understudy had called in sick, and Rupert, in a fit of inspiration or desperation, had insisted Nigel read the part. At first Nigel objected, but within seconds he was reciting *Father Grey*'s cadence, his baritone resonating through the hall.

The crowd, mostly townsfolk pressed into service as extras, erupted in applause. Nigel bowed deeply, one hand to his heart, eyes glittering. For a moment, Freddie saw him not as the washed-up man she'd come to know but as the star Winnie had once adored at the height of his stardom and even on late-night reruns.

Rupert dabbed his eyes with a handkerchief. "The voice of theatrical justice returns to Fernridge!"

Pru muttered to Freddie, "More like the voice of gin and hair pomade." Still, her smile softened as she watched Nigel, her hands pausing over the lemonade pitcher as she poured drinks for the cast.

Freddie leaned back, listening, studying him. His performance was polished, but there was something brittle under the surface. A tremor in the hand, a flicker when the lines hit too close to home.

Then, suddenly, it happened in an instant.

BOOM!

The air above the stage cracked with a sound like a gunshot. A sandbag plummeted from the fly loft, a blur of canvas and weight.

CRASH!

Freddie felt a rush of pain as it grazed her shoulder and then slammed into the floorboards inches from Nigel's feet, the shockwave almost knocking her over. The pain shot down her arm, and she staggered back, Rupert catching her elbow.

Gasps erupted. Someone screamed. The toddler wailed. Rupert thundered, "Curtain! Curtain!" though there was none actually to drop.

Nigel stood frozen, chalk-pale, staring at the bag that could have crushed both of us. His lips moved soundlessly before he crumpled into a chair, shaking.

Freddie pressed her hand to her shoulder. It throbbed, but she was okay. If the bag had swung an inch wider, her stomach turned.

Rupert roared for order, but the auditorium was chaos: actors crowding, townsfolk shouting, Pru pushing over chairs to reach Freddie.

From the back of the room, Deputy Barrett strode forward, hands on her hips, her eyes sharp as glass. Freddie didn't even know she was in the building, but she supposed that was a great trait for law enforcement – always present but rarely seen.

"Clear the stage," Deputy Barrett barked. Her voice cut through the ruckus like a whip. "Everyone off, now."

Grumbling, muttering, people shuffled aside. She bent over the fallen sandbag, fingers probing the rope. When she straightened, her expression was steel.

"Cut," she said flatly. "Clean slice. Box cutter or knife. Not an accident."

A collective gasp rippled through the room. The old woman with pins in her mouth clutched her chest as the pins scattered across the floor. Someone whispered, "The theatre's cursed."

Rupert flung his scarf dramatically over his shoulder. "Cursed, my dear, is the absence of art. This—" He pointed to the rope.—"this is sabotage!"

Barrett shot him a look. "Don't start." She turned to Nigel, still trembling. "Mr. Ashcroft, were you the target?"

Nigel blinked, swallowing hard. "I—I can't say. Perhaps. Or Miss March here. She was quite near also."

All eyes swung to Freddie, causing heat to creep up her neck. She shook her head. "It doesn't matter who. What matters is someone wanted to hurt someone."

Deputy Barrett's jaw tightened. "And I've told you before, Miss March, leave the investigating to me. This is my case, not yours."

The rehearsal was called off, and the set was left half-finished. Townsfolk drifted into the lobby, whispering theories, everything from vengeful spirits to rival drama clubs.

Pru knelt beside Freddie, gently probing her shoulder. "You're gonna bruise. We should ice it."

"I'm fine," Freddie insisted, though her arm throbbed. Her gaze slid to Nigel, seated stiffly with Pru's lemon bar in one hand, untouched. His fingers trembled too much to hold it steady.

For once, he didn't posture. His face was ashen, eyes far away. When Pru placed her hand over his, he startled, then stilled. "Thank you," he whispered hoarsely.

Freddie's suspicion wavered. This wasn't guilt, it was fear. The kind of fear that gnawed at the bones.

Deputy Barrett reappeared, rope in hand. She dropped it onto a folding chair. The end was sliced clean, fibers neat as if cut with scissors.

"This wasn't kids fooling around," she said. "This was deliberate."

Rupert groaned dramatically. "The spirit of Agatha herself walks among us."

Deputy Barrett rolled her eyes but ignored him. Her gaze pinned Freddie. "I mean it. Stay out of this, or next time you won't be so lucky."

Aggie, who wasn't far from Freddie's side these days had slipped in unnoticed, padded onto the stage. He sniffed the rope end, whiskers twitching. Then he let out a grand, wheezy sneeze that echoed across the auditorium.

Laughter broke the tension for a heartbeat. Rupert clutched his scarf. "The feline declares, he has solved the mystery!"

Aggie strutted toward Freddie, plopping down with a huff on top of her foot, as though insulted by the inferior human deduction skills.

Freddie allowed herself a thin smile, but the knot in her stomach didn't ease. Someone had tried to harm them—her, Nigel, maybe both. And whoever it was had access, skill, and desperation.

When the crowd thinned, Freddie lingered in the aisle. Nigel sat slumped, his usual polish fraying. She lowered herself beside him.

"You alright?" she asked softly.

He exhaled shakily. "I once thought the worst thing a fan could do was misquote a line of *Father Grey*. But this..." He shivered. "This is obsession. This is... punishment."

"For what?" Freddie pressed.

He glanced at her, eyes clouded. "For sins I don't even remember committing." He laughed bitterly. "Perhaps for daring to still be alive when Winifred isn't."

Freddie swallowed hard. His words clung to her as Pru rejoined them, fussing, trying to lighten the mood. But Freddie's thoughts were elsewhere, on the sandbag, on the cut rope, on the cold certainty that the limping man was still watching, still waiting.

And for the first time, she wondered if Fernridge itself was the stage for the deadliest play yet.

Back at the bookstore that night, the quiet pressed in like a second skin. The Marple & Quill always seemed gentler after hours, the lamps casting honey-colored pools of light, the shelves looming in rows like old sentinels, but tonight, the hush felt different. Heavier. Waiting.

Freddie let the bolt click shut behind her and stood for a moment, shoulder aching from the sandbag's graze. She could still hear the sharp crack of the rope, the startled gasps from the crowd, and see Nigel's trembling hands afterward. The sound replayed itself in her mind, a loop she couldn't silence.

She set her bag down on the counter, next to the register Winnie had always insisted was "quirky" rather than "temperamental," and pressed a cold pack against the bruise blooming along her collarbone. The sting made her wince, but she welcomed the pain; it grounded her, kept her from spinning too far into fear.

Aggie hopped onto the counter with surprising grace for his girth, his paws landing soft as punctuation marks. He studied her with solemn green eyes, tail curling around his body like a comma. Then, as if making a judgment, he flopped down directly atop Winnie's folder.

"I know," Freddie murmured, stroking his fur. "I shouldn't keep it out in the open."

She nudged him gently aside, earning a theatrical flick of his tail, and drew the folder closer. Inside, Winnie's handwriting snaked across pages: notes, timelines, sketches that made the past feel alive. Freddie took a clean sheet of paper and, in her own neat hand, added a new entry:

Sandbag with rope cut clean. Attempted sabotage? Target: Nigel (or me?). Too deliberate to be accident. Limper desperate?

She underlined the word *desperate* twice, the pen digging into the page.

Her hand hovered. She wanted to write more, to untangle the threads that had brought her here. *Why Nigel? Why now?* The fan letter, the postmark, the church bell, Daniel March's disappearance, all the lines converged on Fernridge like rivers feeding one dark well.

And now someone was trying to silence them.

She pushed back from the counter, pacing the aisles. Her footsteps echoed against the wood floors. The books seemed to lean in, spines whispering. This shop had been her grandmother's pride, her refuge, her stage. To Freddie, it was both sanctuary and cage, every corner saturated with Winnie's absence, and yet every corner reminding her of what she was fighting to preserve.

A floorboard creaked near the back door.

Freddie froze, breath caught in her throat. Aggie's ears pricked forward, body stiffening like a coiled spring. She gripped the edge of the counter, listening.

Another sound, the faintest brush, like something slipping against the doorframe. She grabbed the iron key from the register drawer and crossed to the door, heart hammering.

When she threw it open, the alley yawned back at her, wet and glistening under the guttering streetlamp. Empty. Just the rain dripping steadily from the eaves.

Still, the certainty lingered that someone had been there.

She shut the door, locking the bolt twice this time, and returned to the counter. Aggie leapt back onto Winnie's folder, curling tightly around it. His purr rumbled low, steady, almost like a vow.

Freddie sank into the chair, exhaustion tugging at her, but her resolve burned sharper than before. "I won't stop, Winnie," she whispered, voice barely carrying beyond the pool of lamplight. "Not until I know. Not until I've seen it through. I owe you that much."

A MURDER MOST UNSOLVED

Aggie lifted his head, blinked slowly, and tucked his nose back into his fur, as if sealing the promise between them.

For the first time, Freddie realized the danger wasn't circling the edges anymore. It was inside the borders of her life now, closer than she dared admit. And she wasn't sure who would make the next move, her, or the shadows waiting just beyond the door.

19

FELLOWSHIP AND FUN

The green in front of St. Mary's had never looked so alive.

Sunlight pooled between the elms where bright paper lanterns swung in lazy arcs, waiting for evening to show them off. Quilts and folding chairs dotted the grass like patchwork. Long tables sagged with casseroles, bowls of potato salad, Pru's lemon bars and butter tarts, and a mysterious crockpot that steamed ominously but smelled divine. Someone had strung a banner between the lampposts that read in slightly crooked letters:

FERNRIDGE FUN & FELLOWSHIP DAY

Children chased each other across the lawn with bubble wands, the air filling with iridescent globes that drifted upward and popped against the lantern strings. Older townsfolk staked out chairs in clusters, gossip flowing more freely than the iced tea.

And under the dessert table, like a furry deity holding court, Aggie sprawled on his side with his cream colored belly exposed, smugly collecting pats and sneaked offerings of ham rolls. Luckily, the bookstore was within walking distance to all the high-profile places in Fernridge, so Aggie got to venture out often — way more often than Freddie preferred, actually. He was a menace to keep up with.

Freddie slowed at the edge of the gathering, blinking at the bustle of it all. It felt like stepping into a painting she didn't know she'd been missing.

"Welcome to Fernridge Fun and Fellowship," Pru announced, sweeping her arm like a Price is Right Barker's Beauty as she and Freddie stepped onto the green. "I told you this would cheer you up. Fellowship and Fun is just code for carbs and eavesdropping."

Freddie had resisted coming, the way a waning tide resists a shore, but Pru had insisted in that gentle, relentless Pru way, pressing a lemon bar into Freddie's palm and saying, "Eat and walk."

Freddie gave a small laugh. "I think Aggie already knows that."

As if on cue, Aggie rolled, caught a paper napkin in his claws, and began shredding it with lazy satisfaction. A small crowd of admiring children applauded.

He wore a ruddy ribbon someone had tied around his neck, looped badly, into a bow that sat off-center like a mischievous grin. He paused to let two small children pet him with reverence, then flopped beneath the tablecloth in a puddle of orange fluff, ready to serve as inscrutable guardian of all tasty treats.

Under the largest oak, Father Keating presided over the tea urn, sleeves rolled to the forearms, collar crisp above a plain black shirt. He had the kind of steady, amused face that made people confess to things like stealing hydrangea cuttings and keeping library books past their due dates. As he handed a cup to an elderly gentleman, he added two sugar packets without being asked, the skill of a server who already knew his audience.

When he spotted Freddie and Pru, he lifted his chin in welcome.

"Miss March! Ms. Hawthorn. I'm glad you came. Tea?"

"Yes, thank you," Freddie said, stepping closer. "Your parish has outdone itself."

The priest smiled with a knowing head nod and handed her a cup with both hands, steady as stone. "Oh, it's not my parish, Miss March. It's theirs. I just try to keep the lights on and not to step on any toes."

Freddie moved to take a sip, and Father Keating added, "Be warned, it's strong enough to strip varnish. Mrs. Clemons insisted we make it double."

Pru sniffed the steam and said dryly, "One sip and you'll remember your sins from kindergarten."

Father Keating chuckled. "Then it's doing half my job for me."

A woman with hair the color of strawberry jam hustled by carrying a casserole labeled **SUSPICIOUSLY LIKE LASAGNA**. "Don't worry," she told no one in particular, "it's vegetarian if you pick out the sausage."

"That's Miss Tansy Dell," Pru whispered. "She will sing later. She doesn't have to, and no one will enjoy it, but she will."

"Bless her," Father Keating said, a hint of mischief in his eyes. "We keep a spare microphone and a sense of humor."

On the far end of the green, Mr. Clyde Harlan stood proudly beside his annual raffle item: a hand-carved wooden goose with a slightly villainous glint in its painted eyes. A sign read **WIN THIS BEAUTY!** Beneath it, in smaller letters: **NO RETURNS**. Children circled it with the wary respect owed to cursed artifacts.

Kevin appeared with a stack of paper plates and a trail of admiration from three teenage girls who absolutely didn't notice they were staring. "Pru, the blueberry crumb bars are disappearing like a government file," he reported. "Also, Aggie stole a napkin and is refusing to give it back. He's made it a hostage situation."

"Offer him diplomatic immunity," Pru said, waving him off. "And keep the cookie line moving. If Miss Ada and Miss June have to wait for snickerdoodles, they'll unionize."

Freddie watched it all with a soft ache. This was what she'd missed, without even knowing she was missing it: a place where people had favorite folding chairs and jokes about pies that went back decades. A place where you could say someone's name and five stories would rise to meet it.

"Come," Father Keating said, balancing two teas with ease. "Let's claim some grass before the hymn bingo starts."

They carried their cups to a quilt beneath the oak, where Father Keating settled cross-legged despite the protest of his knees. "Don't let anyone rope me into softball again," he said. "Last year, I fouled the ball and hit the choir director. Nearly had to absolve myself on the spot."

Freddie laughed, genuinely, the kind that made her ribs unclench.

Everywhere she looked, Fernridge unspooled its odd little charms.

Miss Dell commandeered the microphone from the youth band and launched into an old ballad three keys too high. No one seemed to mind though. People clapped along, indulgent.

Mr. Clyde Harlan strutted from picnic table to picnic table trying his best to sell raffle tickets for his goose. "One dollar a ticket!" he barked. "She'll guard your house from burglars and geese alike." Most people laughed, and some happily purchased.

Two freckled twins began a three-legged race at the far side of the green. They managed five triumphant steps before collapsing in a heap of tangled limbs and delighted shrieks.

Freddie watched it all, and something pooled warm inside her chest. The town wasn't polished, but it was stubbornly itself. Slowly and with great hesitation, she was beginning to feel like it might have room for her, too.

"We're dedicating tonight to Winifred," Father Keating said quietly. "At the close, before we light the lanterns. She insisted we call this 'fun and fellowship' when I floated 'fellowship and fun.' 'Put fun first,' she said. 'People will forgive anything, Father, if you feed them and make them laugh.'"

Freddie's throat pinched. "That sounds like her."

"It was her," he said, then studied Freddie's face for a moment with a gentleness that invited truth. "How are you holding up?"

The natural answer of *fine* rose to her lips and fell, rightly, away. "Holding," she said instead. "Sometimes by the corners."

He nodded, as if that were a holy practice. "Sometimes that's all any of us can manage."

A glint of silver caught her eye: Deputy Barrett's cruiser, parked just off the curb. The deputy herself strode the perimeter of the gathering, her boots making efficient arcs across the grass. Her expression was the same sharp one Freddie had seen in TV show interrogations, focused and unreadable. Then a kid in a superhero cape ran straight up to the deputy and offered her a cookie. Deputy Barrett tried not to smile but failed miserably.

"Deputy," Father Keating called. "You're just in time. We were about to debate the theological implications of snickerdoodles."

She deadpanned, "I'll enter it into the record," but her eyes crinkled.

"Hi, Lila," Pru said cheerfully. "Here to ticket illegal lemonade vendors?"

"Only if they're charging more than market rate," she replied. She glanced at Freddie, reading her with that level, weighing gaze. "Can we talk a minute?"

"Of course," Freddie said, heart hitching.

They stepped just beyond the lantern string, into a sliver of shade that smelled like freshly cut grass and a hint of rain that wasn't there yet. Deputy Barrett rested one hand on her belt, the posture of a woman choosing words carefully.

"Off duty, I would say nothing here," she began. "On duty, I have to say something. The theatre, the rope. You get that whoever did that isn't playing. Right?"

Freddie nodded.

"I'm not telling you to stop breathing," Deputy Barrett said, softer now. "But I am telling you that if you plan to chase anything, I need to know where. Even if it's 'I'm going to chase a pie.'"

Freddie tried to pull on a smile that came out crooked. "Pru would chase a pie."

"Pru would make the pie chase her," she said, almost smiling herself. "Look. Winnie was...good to a lot of people. Me included. She loaned me detective novels when I was a kid and said, 'Here. Read these and find the plot holes.' I owe her. And I plan to repay that debt the right way." She tipped her chin toward the lanterns, the church, the town. "Let me do my job."

Freddie felt the old instinct to hold everything tight in her chest. But Deputy Barrett's edges didn't feel like fences; they felt like guardrails.

"I will," Freddie said. "And, thank you."

Lila nodded once, formal and real. Then the superhero-caped kid returned to stick a star sticker on the deputy's sleeve. She looked down at it like it had appeared by magic, nodded her head, and then left it.

When Freddie returned to the quilt, Father Keating had produced a tin of butter cookies from somewhere in his clerical bag. He offered it wordlessly; she took one.

For several minutes, they watched the quiet theatre of the town. Kevin demonstrated a card trick to a flock of middle-schoolers. Pru and Mr. Harlan argued happily about the correct diameter of a cobbler crust. Miss Tansy attempted harmony with herself.

The talk around them flowed to small things, who'd seen the first fireflies of the season, whether the community garden's tomatoes were more confident this year, and the smallness steadied Freddie in a way a large gesture never could. Her shoulders lowered. Her breath remembered its purpose.

"Father," she said at last, and the word felt less formal than it had an hour ago. "I've been…looking into things. Some of the things Winnie was looking into. I don't know if it's wrong to do that. Or foolish. But it feels like something that lets me breathe."

He looked at her fondly, not surprised by her confession. "Tell me the parts you can tell."

Freddie told him—not all of it, not the names or the worst leaps, but the shape of her fear and the outline of her pursuit. She mentioned the hollowed-out book, the sketch of a limping stance, the chain Winnie had underlined: bell, stoplight, missing man. She admitted she'd gone to the library archives, that Pru had come with her, that Penny from the Motor Court had said a name she couldn't shake. She did not say Daniel March, but the absence of the name lay between them like a small stone.

Father Keating listened as if his vocation were simply to be a sturdy chair, which she figured it kind of was. When she finished, he didn't rush to fill the silence. He let it be what it was, a vessel between them.

"Mysteries thrive in silence," he said finally, his voice as even as a level. "But not all silences are the same. Some are grief—good, necessary, heavy as quilts. Some are fear—useful at the edge of a roof or a cliff. And some are guilt—thin, but sticky." His mouth curved. "The trick is telling which is which before you trip over the wrong one."

Freddie huffed a soft laugh. "I knew you were going to say something like that. Sage advice, helpful but not really helpful."

"I am suspiciously consistent," he agreed. "Two thoughts, Miss March. First, write everything down in ink. Memory is a trickster. Write the facts and your thoughts about them, the whole picture. The page can hold what your heart can't. Second, when you ask questions, try to offer people a way to tell the truth without losing face. Give them dignity. You can pull a thread without tearing the whole sweater."

"That last one sounds like you've done this before."

"Parish life is ninety percent sweater maintenance," he said gravely. Then his gaze gentled even more. "You remind me of Winifred when she was at her sharpest. She cut right to the heart of a thing, but she never made the heart bleed."

Freddie swallowed hard.

"And if you want practical help," he added lightly, "our parish bulletins from the late '90s are boxed in the church basement. Donations, fundraiser notes, and lists of who fixed things. Not exactly police records, but sometimes they tell the broader story."

"You'd let me look?"

"I'd watch you look," he said. "There's a difference." He winked. "But yes."

Aggie, as if on cue, stood and stretched, then padded delicately onto Father Keating's knee and made himself a cat-shaped paperweight.

"Ah," the priest said, unmoving while Aggie kneaded his thigh. "I have been chosen."

"That's the highest office in town," Pru said, dropping to the quilt with a plate of deviled eggs and an expression of triumph. "Eat or I revoke your fellowship."

Freddie took a deviled egg and bit into it. Paprika, cream, mustard. The taste was so sincerely excellent she nearly cried.

"Who made these?" she asked through a full, reverent mouth.

"Miss June," Pru said. "She says the secret is love and a terrifying amount of salt."

Father Keating leaned back on his hands. "Before we light the lanterns, I'll say a word for Winifred. Nothing long." He tilted his head at Freddie. "Would that be alright?"

Freddie surprised herself again by laughing. "If you say 'nothing long,' you will most certainly jinx it to be long."

"I'll risk it," he said with a wink.

Someone, mercifully, took back the microphone from Miss Tansy and gave it to the youth group, who rendered "This Little Light of Mine" as if it were a fight song.

A MURDER MOST UNSOLVED

Dusk became the kind of blue that made white shirts glow and faces look like they'd been brushed with fairy water.

Father Keating stood, Aggie dismounting with a polite chirp, and climbed the parish hall stoop. He didn't need to call for quiet; it arrived, a gentle tide, as the hymn ended and the town turned to listen.

"Friends," he said, not using the microphone, because he didn't need it. "We said we'd put the fun first, and we have. And now we will keep our promise to fellowship." He glanced toward the lanterns, still blank and expectant above us. "This evening is for Winifred March, who taught us a thousand small ways to be good to each other. She stocked the mysteries and solved not a few. She believed, against all evidence sometimes, that people could surprise you for the better."

A ripple of low laughter—soft, rueful, fond—moved across the green.

"She also believed," he went on, "that light is meant to be shared. Not hoarded. Not hidden." He nodded at the row of lanterns. "When we light these in a moment, I'd invite you to hold in your heart one good thing she gave you. A book. A word. A look that said, 'I see you.' Then carry that forward. That is the work. Not grand gestures but daily gestures of kindness."

He paused, and for a beat Freddie thought he might tip over into sadness. But he didn't. He steadied, like a man finding his balance on a small boat.

"And if you are new to our town—" his eyes flickered to Freddie for just a heartbeat, a kindness without calling her out—"you should know: we mean it. You belong as you show up. Show up enough and you'll find yourself held."

Pru sniffed loudly and claimed it was the deviled eggs.

The first lantern blinked on, then the second, then the third. A string of small suns lifted the green into an amber glow, soft and steady. Someone sighed loudly. Children reached up as if they could pocket the light.

Freddie tipped her head back and let the glow write itself across her face. She felt a loosening in her chest that had nothing to do with solving anything and everything to do with being seen in a place that remembered how life should be.

Aggie bonked her ankle with his head, then launched himself gracefully into Father Keating's lap again just as he retook his spot on the quilt, this time with a single commanding chirp, as if to say, sit still; receive.

Freddie did. She sat still. She received all that Winnie was giving her by extension of Fernridge.

Beside her, Pru threaded her fingers through Freddie's for a second and squeezed, no words needed. Farther off, Deputy Barrett watched the edges of the green the way a good guardian watches a sleeping house—alert, present, softer than steel but steel all the same.

And Freddie, who had come to Fernridge to answer a letter and found a life she hadn't thought she was allowed to want, decided that tomorrow could bring whatever it wanted. Tonight, there were lanterns and lemon bars and a priest who kept butter cookies in his pocket and a cat who always knew exactly the right thing to do.

For the first time in too long, the quiet inside her wasn't fear. It was belonging.

20

DEADLY FAIRY CASTLES

The morning after Fernridge Fun and Fellowship, the world felt almost too gentle. Which, if Freddie was being honest, felt like a harbinger of doom, though she tried hard to ward off that feeling.

Sunlight poured through the wide front windows of The Marple & Quill, painting warm squares across the bookstore floorboards. Freddie sat cross-legged behind the counter, a pencil caught between her teeth as she sorted through a stack of new arrivals. Aggie sprawled belly-up beside her, pawing at the twirling string from the paper bundle.

For the first time since arriving in Fernridge, Freddie's chest wasn't a stone. It was still heavy, yes, but last night's lanterns had left something inside her loosened, like the first sigh after holding one's breath too long. She could still see the way the little globes of light had swayed in the trees, still hear Father Keating's voice carrying across the green, still feel Pru's hand threading through hers with wordless solidarity.

She hadn't realized how badly she'd needed to belong somewhere. Probably because she didn't really know what it felt like to belong until today.

She flipped her notebook open and started a new list, her handwriting looping with more steadiness than before:

Things I Can Control:

- Shelve the poetry section (Winnie's favorites on display).

- Have one of Pru's lemon bars for breakfast (for medicinal purposes).

- Keep asking questions, quietly.

- Do not, under any circumstances, adopt a second cat.

Aggie batted at the pencil stub, as if disagreeing with number four. Freddie smiled, tapped his nose, and scratched behind his ears.

The little bell over the door jingled, and Deputy Barrett stepped inside.

Her boots sounded too sharp against the creaky wooden planks, and the smile Freddie had been nurturing thinned. The doom had seemingly arrived right on time. The deputy wasn't in her "fellowship mode" from last night, softened by children and pie. Today she wore her full armor: pressed uniform, duty belt glinting, expression set to professional neutrality.

"Miss March."

Freddie rose, her knees stiff from the floor. "Deputy. Good morning."

Deputy Barrett glanced at Aggie, who offered her a slow blink of disdain, then back to Freddie. Her lips pressed into a line. "I need a word."

Something in the tone made Freddie's stomach dip. She gestured to the armchairs near the mystery shelves. "Of course. Sit?"

Deputy Barrett didn't. She stayed standing, arms loose at her sides but eyes unwavering.

"The toxicology report came back."

The sentence landed like a boulder breaking glass. Freddie's skin prickled. "Oh." Her throat tightened. "And?"

Deputy Barrett inhaled slowly, as if even she didn't want to shape the words. "Digitalis. Extract from foxglove. A lethal dose."

The word snagged in Freddie's chest. *Foxglove.* Her mind didn't just hear it, it smelled it, sweet, faintly bitter, the way Winnie's garden used to smell on June mornings. She saw herself at six years old, sitting in the grass while Winnie knelt beside the flowerbeds. "Pretty bells," she had called them, reaching to pluck one. Winnie had caught her hand midair. "Not for touching, darling. These are fairy castles, but they're dangerous ones. They look kind, but they can stop a heart in an instant. Freddie remembered laughing then, skipping away, forgetting the warning as children do. But now it thundered through her skull—deadly fairy castles. And someone had used them on Winnie.

The bookstore tilted. Freddie gripped the arm of the chair, nails digging into the wood. "But foxglove? That's just flowers. Gardens."

"It's common," Deputy Barrett said carefully, "and that makes it dangerous. Easy to overlook. Easy to use."

Freddie's voice broke, sharper than she intended. "So it wasn't natural."

"No," Deputy Barrett said. "It was deliberate. Someone staged it to appear peaceful, complete with tea and a book. But it wasn't natural causes."

Freddie's hand clamped over her mouth. A hot sting built behind her eyes, but tears wouldn't fall; they burned instead, like smoke caught inside her. All she could see was her grandmother in that armchair, the cup balanced at her side, the quiet repose. It hadn't been repose at all.

It had been murder.

She let her head fall into her hands while she gathered herself then looked back at the deputy. "She suffered," she whispered. "Did she—did she know?"

Deputy Barrett's gaze softened just enough to acknowledge the question without drowning in it. "Digitalis can slow the heart. It can look like faintness, tiredness. Then it stops the rhythm. We can't say exactly what she felt. But I wouldn't think it was prolonged."

Freddie pressed her palms to her eyes. The thought was unbearable, and yet the knowledge was worse if she didn't face it. "She trusted someone enough to drink the tea they gave her."

Deputy Barrett's jaw flexed. "Maybe." She let that hang a beat before adding, "Miss March, I need you to understand something clearly. This isn't a puzzle in a book. This is someone in Fernridge. Someone who took the time to plan, to poison, to cover their tracks. They may still be here. And they are not playing."

Freddie's grief snapped white-hot into focus, burning through her veins. "Then I'll find them."

"You won't," Deputy Barrett said flatly. "You'll let me and my department find them."

Freddie lifted her head, anger crackling. "Winnie deserves—"

"Justice," Deputy Barrett cut in. "And she'll get it. But not from you charging blind into every shadow. I'm telling you now: stop investigating. For your own safety. Winnie deserves for her killer to be found, but she does not deserve for her only granddaughter to get herself killed in the process."

Freddie barely heard her until the deputy's voice sharpened. "This isn't one of your mysteries in a book, this is real life."

And in that moment, Freddie remembered Father Keating last night, his eyes crinkled kindly over the rim of his teacup. *"Mysteries thrive in silence. The trick is knowing which silence is grief, and which is guilt."* Was this what he'd meant? That the hush over Fernridge wasn't just sorrow, it was secrecy. She could almost hear his voice urging her: *Write it down, Miss March. The page can hold what your heart can't.* Her throat ached. She wasn't ready to write it down yet, not ready for it to be that real – in print. But the seed had been planted.

The door burst open so hard it jammed and didn't close behind her. Pru breezed in, arms full of a bakery box, humming something off-key. "Good morning, my bookish ducklings! I've brought reinforcements in the form of—"

She stopped dead.

Her gaze swept from Deputy Barrett's stiff posture to Freddie's blotchy face, to the silence that had thickened the air. She set the box down too hard, baked goods scattering against the cardboard walls. "What happened?"

Deputy Barrett answered before Freddie could. "It's official. Winifred March was poisoned."

Pru's hands curled on the counter. For once, humor deserted her. "Poisoned."

"Yes," Deputy Barrett said.

Freddie's voice came rough, broken. "Foxglove. Fairy castles," she only managed to croak out.

Something flickered in Pru's eyes—shock, then fury, then a brittle kind of grief she covered almost immediately with a mask. She moved around the the furniture and Deputy Barrett and put both hands on Freddie's shoulders. "Breathe. In and out. That's all you've got to do right now."

Freddie shook her head and stood swiftly to her feet. "I can't just sit here."

Pru's mouth twisted. "No one's asking you to sit," she said as she pushed Freddie back into her chair. "But maybe don't run headlong into whoever thought poisoning your grandmother was a good idea."

"You heard the deputy," Freddie said bitterly.

"I did." Pru squeezed her shoulders. "So we'll just have to investigate smarter, harder."

Deputy Barrett's gaze flicked toward Pru. "This isn't a game."

"No," Pru shot back, arms crossed, chin tilted high with resolve. "But neither is losing someone who mattered more than your own skin. So, unless you're planning to lock us in a cell, Deputy, maybe you ought to accept that Freddie and I aren't going to sit quietly knitting doilies while you chase paperwork."

Deputy Barrett's nostrils flared. For a heartbeat, Freddie thought she'd actually arrest Pru for sass alone. But then—so faint Freddie almost doubted it—she saw a flicker of something soften in the deputy's eyes. Respect, maybe. Or recognition.

"At least promise me you'll tell me where you're poking. I can't stop you from whispering to each other, but I can stop you from walking into the lion's mouth."

Freddie swallowed hard, nodding. "Fine. I promise."

Mrs. Callahan, the neighbor from down the lane, tottered in the open door, smelling faintly of rosewater. She clutched a basket of rhubarb and lowered her voice conspiratorially, not caring that she was giving away her eavesdropping. "You'll want to know, I saw that actor man—Mr. Nigel Ashcroft—buying tea the other night. Late. Right before closing. Looked awfully particular about the blend."

Freddie blinked, her stomach twisting. "Nigel?"

Mrs. Callahan nodded with satisfaction, as if delivering freshly baked gossip. "Yes. Just thought you ought to know." She deposited the rhubarb on the counter and swept out again, leaving a swirl of perfume and suspicion.

Deputy Barrett exhaled sharply through her nose. "Or he was buying for Rupert, or himself, or any one of the hundreds of townsfolk that has tea in their cupboards. Don't go stringing ropes around every leaf bag from the grocer."

But Freddie's mind had already latched onto the image of Nigel at the counter, choosing tea. The same Nigel who had written an episode where a recluse died with tea in his hand. The same Nigel who'd been brought here under Winnie's invitation. Coincidence? Winnie would willingly accept a freshly made cup of tea from Nigel.

Deputy Barrett gave her a look sharp enough to slice bread. "Don't."

Pru looped her arm through Freddie's, tugging her gently toward the back room. "Come on, love. Before you start building murder boards on the poetry shelf. Let's get you upstairs. I'll put the closed sign out and lock up for the day. You've had quite a shock."

Pru forced her to lie down on the couch and promise she'd lie there for at least an hour before she set out on her revenge plot. Then she heard Pru and Deputy Barrett exchange a few heated words before the bell above the door rang upon their exit.

She didn't make it an hour, but she felt 30-ish minutes was ample time to rest after officially finding out your grandmother had been murdered.

Now she was hiding in the storeroom, slumped against the wall. The smell of paper and pastries clung to the air. She thought of last night's lanterns, how she had felt for one fragile moment like she belonged in Fernridge.

Now that same town felt like it was full of shadows.

She closed her eyes. Behind them rose her grandmother's voice, soft but steady: *Put fun first. People will forgive anything, if you feed them and make them laugh.* She recalled the words Father Keating had shared with her just last night but they seemed to have even more meaning today.

Freddie whispered into the quiet, "They took you from me. They made it look peaceful, but it wasn't. And I won't let them hide."

Freddie sat with her notebook open on her knees. She stared at the blank page, pencil trembling. Slowly, she wrote:

Case Notes, Winnie March

Poisoned with digitalis (foxglove)

Scene staged: tea, book, chair

Resembles *Father Grey* episode "A Murder Most Unsolved"

Suspects (so far): ? Nigel (tea purchase?), ? unknown visitor (E. Pike alias)

Her hand shook, but she kept writing, just as Father Keating had advised. Each word steadied her.

Aggie leapt into her lap and sprawled across the page, purring so loudly the pencil rattled. Freddie laughed, a broken sound but real all the same. "Fine, I'll share the credit. Co-investigator: Aggie the Cat."

A MURDER MOST UNSOLVED

She smoothed the fur between his ears, her vision sharpening. They had staged it to look like a story. But stories could be read. And she would read this one until the very last page.

21

THE UNDERWEAR BOOK

The bell over the door jingled so often that morning that Freddie half wondered if it was auditioning for its own role in the town symphony. The Marple & Quill was alive in a way she hadn't yet seen since her return, voices overlapping in the aisles, shoes squeaking on the scuffed oak floor, Aggie sprawled like a lazy monarch in the window seat as if presiding over it all.

Freddie tucked a strand of hair behind her ear and slid the last copy of *The Murder of Roger Ackroyd* into its place. Winnie would have been pleased. Customers milling about the shop, arms heavy with books, it was exactly the sort of hum she'd always cultivated.

"Excuse me, dear," a reedy voice said.

Freddie turned to see Mr. Blanchard, the retired teacher who always carried a faint smell of chalk dust even years after his classroom days. He tapped his cane on the floor like punctuation.

"I need a mystery," he declared. "Crosswords aren't hard enough anymore. They don't fight back like books can."

Freddie smiled. "Do you want a classic puzzle mystery or something more modern?"

"Classic. If there's a dead body in the library, all the better."

She plucked a copy of *The Body in the Library* from the Christie shelf and handed it over.

He chuckled, eyes twinkling. "Agatha and I, we understand each other." He tucked the book under his arm like a prize won.

A few minutes later, the bell chimed again and in slouched Mariah Clarke, fourteen and forever rolling her eyes at the world. She pretended to browse cookbooks while sneaking glances at the fantasy section.

Freddie leaned casually against the shelf. "The new *Dragonblood Saga* just came in."

Mariah's cheeks flushed pink. "I don't read those."

"Of course not," Freddie said solemnly. "I'll just put this copy on the counter in case someone who doesn't read it wants to pick it up later."

Mariah grabbed it so fast her bracelets jingled. "Fine. But if you tell anyone, I'll deny it."

Freddie winked. "Your secret's safe."

Then came Mr. Dale Harper, who always entered the store with a scowl as though books personally offended him. He wandered the shelves muttering under his breath until Freddie asked, "Looking for anything in particular?"

"No," he barked, then five seconds later: "Maybe poetry."

Freddie guided him to a slim volume of Mary Oliver. He bought it gruffly, muttering, "It's not for me." But Freddie caught the way he smoothed the cover before tucking it under his coat, and she remembered whispers that he visited his late wife's grave every Sunday with flowers. Poetry, she realized, was likely meant for her.

The shop settled into a quieter rhythm after that. Freddie straightened the displays, wiped the counter, and tried to memorize the feeling: people laughing, confiding, asking for help with books, as if they were asking for directions back to themselves. She could almost imagine herself doing this forever.

Two women appeared in the aisle like characters stepping off the page of a well-worn book. Mrs. Ada Harwell, neat as pressed linen, and Miss June Pritchard, who looked as though she'd just come from winning the grand prize for her strawberry scones at the county baking competition. They traveled together through Fernridge like twin bookends.

"Freddie dear," Ada said, patting her arm with smooth fingers. "We've come to trouble you."

"That's what I'm here for," Freddie replied, dusting her palms against her skirt.

Ada leaned in. "My great nephew and his new bride are coming to stay. I want something...impressive. They're 'foodies,' you see. They post pictures of starters and drizzles." Her face puckered as if the words themselves tasted odd. "Do you have a cookbook that makes one look sophisticated without being impossible?"

Freddie guided her toward the nonfiction shelves. "I think Winnie set aside a copy of *The Southern Table with a Twist*. It has things like sweet potato gnocchi and lavender lemonade, familiar, but with enough flair to make you look like a genius."

Ada clasped her hands. "Lavender! That will smell refined even if it tastes like soap."

June, meanwhile, had wandered straight to the romance display, her eyes shining. "I need something modern," she announced. "It's been fifty years since I...well. Since anyone took me to dinner." She blushed scarlet but pressed on. "My neighbor lost his wife last winter. He's lonely, and I was thinking—maybe—dinner? But I've forgotten how to go about it."

Freddie stifled a smile. "So you'd like inspiration?"

"Exactly," June said, picking up a paperback with a windswept couple on the cover. "This looks instructional."

Ada snorted. "Instructional? June, that looks like it belongs behind the counter."

But Freddie steered her toward something gentler—*Second Chances at Silverlinings Inn*. "This one's sweet, funny, and the heroine hasn't dated in decades either."

June hugged the book to her chest. "Perfect. If she can figure it out, so can I."

As the women paid, June whispered, "If you hear wedding bells in six months, you'll know why."

"I'll expect an invitation," Freddie said warmly.

The bell jingled again, and this time a young mother appeared, dragging a boy of about eight who looked like he'd been fueled entirely by sugar and comic books.

"Miss March," the mother said breathlessly, "your grandmother told me about a book, something about raising respectful teenagers? I need it sooner than I thought. My daughter is thirteen and has suddenly become..." She lowered her voice. "A fire breathing dragon."

Freddie chuckled. "That would be *Untangled*. Winnie recommended it often." She pulled a copy from the shelf and handed it over.

"Bless you," the mother murmured, clutching it like a lifeline.

Meanwhile, the boy had marched straight up to the counter. "Do you have the underwear book?"

His mother gasped. "Jeremy!"

"*Captain Underpants, Mom!*" He rolled his eyes. "The new one's not out yet, but I still have two left to read first." He said it like a solemn update on national affairs.

Freddie crouched so they were eye to eye. "We have the last two right here. Want me to go ahead and pre-order the next one so you'll get it as soon as it comes out?"

His grin nearly split his face. "Yes, please! You're better than Amazon."

She winked. "Don't tell them that."

The bell rang again, slower this time, as Nigel Ashcroft crept inside. He looked every inch the faded star: tweed jacket too heavy for the weather, hair silvered but stubbornly styled, his smile stretched thin like parchment. He walked the shop as though it belonged to him, fingers trailing along spines, eyes scanning every corner.

"Miss March," he said, voice smooth but just a touch frayed. "Fernridge grows more enchanting by the day."

Freddie kept her tone polite. "Business has been good this morning."

"Good, good." He picked up a copy of the *Father Grey* picture book, studied it, then set it down with exaggerated care. "Still strange to see myself rendered in watercolor. A man should never outlive his own legend."

Freddie said nothing.

Nigel leaned against the counter, eyes narrowing. "Tell me, are you considering staying? Fernridge has its charms, wouldn't you agree? And your mother, will she be joining you?"

Freddie stiffened. "My mother passed away when I was nineteen."

For a heartbeat, Nigel faltered. A shadow flickered across his face before he recovered. "Ah. Tragic. My condolences."

He cleared his throat. "And your father, Daniel March, was it? Curious fellow. What became of him?"

The question landed like a punch in Freddie's gut. "Why do you ask?"

"Idle curiosity. Writers, actors, we are nosy creatures by nature." He smiled, but it didn't touch his eyes.

Freddie's heart pounded. She opened her mouth, ready to demand what he really wanted—

The bell interrupted.

An elderly woman entered, rose scent trailing in with her. "Do you have any of scones left, dear? I'm hosting tea this afternoon."

Freddie forced a smile, packed up the scones, and rang up the sale. When she looked back, Nigel had slipped away, leaving the bell's echo in his wake.

Freddie locked the door early. In the back office, she wrote in her notebook:

Nigel Ashcroft

Probing questions about family (why?)

Reaction to mother's death → suspicious

Why ask about my dad?

She stared at the page until the ink blurred, then flipped open her laptop. Search after search painted the same picture: Nigel Ashcroft had been dropped by his agent years ago after too many drunken scandals. His acting career was nonexistent. The only work he'd done recently was promoting that *Father Grey* picture book in small English bookshops. The photos hurt to look at, Nigel grinning too brightly for too small a crowd.

Something was wrong. Something he wasn't saying.

Later that evening, she went in search of him. She wanted to confront him about why he was asking so many questions, especially about her dad, but she also had finally gotten up the nerve to ask about his connection to all of this. She found him at the playhouse, backstage in a green room that contained a futon bed and was littered with empty bottles. The smell of whiskey and dust clung to the air.

"Nigel," she said softly.

He looked up, eyes glassy. "Miss March! Have you come to cast me? I can still play a young lover, with the right lighting."

She sat across from him. "I wanted to ask about the *Father Grey* episode, 'A Murder Most Unsolved.'"

He launched into the plot with drunken bravado: the old recluse, the book, the tea, the bells. Freddie listened but heard nothing new.

Finally, his shoulders slumped. "Truth is, I'm finished and washed up. Even Rupert won't give me the lead in *And Then There Were None*. Imagine! Me, begging for scraps. I was someone once."

Freddie's chest ached, but before she could respond he muttered thickly, "It's all my fault."

She leaned forward. "What is?"

But his eyes had closed, his words dissolving into unconsciousness. Freddie pulled a blanket over his shoulders, then stood in the doorway, watching the once-great actor crumble into snores.

A MURDER MOST UNSOLVED

The words followed her out into the night like a shadow:
It's all my fault.

22

God's Attic

It was another day of storms rolling into Fernridge like a diva actress making an entrance, loud, deliberate, and impossible to ignore. Thunder hammered at the windows of The Marple & Quill until the glass hummed. Rain streamed down the panes in rough, silver cords. Every flash of lightning turned the rows of books into stark ribs, then snatched them back to shadow. The brass bell over the door quivered on its hook, though no one touched it.

Freddie sat at the counter with her notebook open and her pen uncapped, the page wet from her damp sleeve where the open window had spit. She kept glancing up toward the far end of Main Street, where the church spire sometimes strobed into existence when lightning ripped through the sky.

Winnie's handwriting pulsed in her mind: **Storm → Bell/stoplight → Missing man.** Freddie tapped her pen on the paper while she kept repeating the words in her head, willing them to give her some great epiphany about this whole thing.

Aggie sprawled like a living comma beside her notebook, chin on the paper as if he could create additional notes by sheer feline will.

With each tap tap, his tail flicked once, judgmental, weary. Freddie reached and rubbed the soft crease between his ears.

"Don't you dare," Pru said from behind the pastry case without looking up. She was repackaging scones into neat twine-tied bundles even though, realistically, no rational person would come out in this weather for a pastry. "That look on your face? That's your 'I'm about to run headlong into danger' look—you had it at ten years old too."

Freddie swallowed. "I need to check the church tower tonight."

Pru slapped the twine against the counter, then bounced it twice to settle. "Why do we even stage a talk where I say 'let's use our brains' and you say 'let's climb into a lightning rod during a lightning storm' if we both know how it ends?"

"Winnie had the bell circled," Freddie said. She could hear her own voice going quiet and stubborn, the way it always did when a thought had moved from idea to necessity. "If there's something up there, I won't sleep until I know."

"Darling," Pru said, softening, "you're not sleeping anyway."

Before Freddie could answer, the door shouldered itself inward on a gust and Nigel stumbled in, soaked through to his shirt. He looked less like a star and more like a man who'd been dragged down the block by weather and pride. His scarf clung to his neck like it had lost a fight with a drainpipe. His eyes, though, were clear and steady.

"We're going," Freddie added as her final decision on the matter.

Pru huffed.

"You're not going without me," he said, voice pitched low enough to be a vow.

Pru made a face of theatrical suffering. "Of course not. The washed-up wanna-be British priest joins the suicide squad when he doesn't even know where we're going."

Nigel peeled off his coat with dignity. "The washed-up *crime-solving* British priest, Prudence, so I'm not completely useless. And where you go, I go." He placed his hand over his heart and bowed his head.

"Actor, washed-up actor," Freddie mumbled but was ignored.

"Useful would be 'owns a boat,'" Pru muttered and pointed to the flooding streets out the front glass. "Or 'knows how to file restraining orders against ghosts.'"

Nigel's gaze flicked to the window, to the spire briefly illuminated in the next flash, and then to Freddie. "Winnie wanted answers," he said. "We owe her courage."

Freddie looked toward Pru then pointed her pen at Nigel. "He seems to know too much."

Pru shrugged. "We had a talk after your encounter yesterday, he's now up to speed."

Freddie rolled her eyes but supposed she couldn't blame Nigel for seeking out Pru nor Pru for confiding in Nigel. Winnie was her best friend, and Pru had been such a source of strength, but she knew deep down it was hard on her too.

Aggie sneezed as if to say: this is all very stirring; also, your scarf smells like pond water.

A mere ten minutes later, Pru's station wagon plowed through a shallow river that Fernridge called Elder Lane, the windshield wipers sawing back and forth like a metronome losing its patience. The streetlights wore cones of rain. Trash bins rolled in slow, apologetic circles at the curb. Freddie braced her hand on the dash as the car crested a rising sheet of water and the tires found purchase on the slick.

"Last chance to say this is a terrible idea," Pru offered, knuckles white on the wheel.

"It is a terrible idea," Nigel said from the back seat. "We're still going."

Freddie gave a small, unsteady laugh, which made her feel braver than she was.

St. Mary's loomed against the sky, its steeple a black stitch in the seam of the storm. Wind shoved at them as soon as they opened the car doors, turning umbrellas into bright, defeated tulips. They ran for the shelter of the portico, their shoes slapping flat, rain leaping from the stone in wild rebounds.

Inside, the nave breathed cold and dim. Candlewax and old wood and lingering incense, Freddie's lungs recognized it before her mind did. Lightning flashed through stained glass, and saints flickered in crimson and cobalt, then dissolved again into shadow. Water ticked from a far corner, steady as a clock.

"Father Keating?" Pru called softly. Only their echoes answered. "Just checking," she whispered to her foolish companions.

Freddie's light found the side door that led up into the tower. The paint at the latch was blistered; the metal, a little rusty. Lightning strobed again and she saw the rope. A thick, woolly length that rose into darkness. It bumped softly against its pulley as if the storm were testing the bell.

"Up," Nigel said, under his breath. "Quickly."

The stairwell was a stone spiral, tight and damp. Freddie's phone flashlight fanned the steps into being one at a time, as though they were newly appearing just ahead of her shoe. The air tightened with each turn, the storm's roar compressing into a low, omnipresent growl. She counted the steps to calm herself—twenty-two, twenty-three, twenty-four—until counting felt like inviting a misstep.

Nigel trailed a step behind Pru, one hand on the center column. He tried to make it look gallant; she could hear his quickened breath. "I hate heights," he admitted into the back of Pru's coat, the confession startlingly human. "Stage catwalks are one thing. God's attic is another."

"Good news," Pru said. "If you faint, she and I will drag you by your scarf."

The trapdoor at the top was a square of darkness. Freddie balanced the phone between her teeth and pushed with her shoulder. It stuck, then gave with a crack and a burst of colder air that smelled of wet rope and pigeon poo and something metallic. Lightning raked the slatted louvers, and the space popped bright, then went black again, leaving the bell as a ghost imprint in Freddie's dark eyesight.

The tower chamber was a rib cage of beams. The great bronze bell loomed above them, slicked by humidity, its lip beaded. Ropes hung in slow arcs, swaying to the storm's will. Somewhere a bird made a disgruntled sound at their unwelcome presence.

"Careful," Pru said. "If we die, I'm haunting both of you."

"You can't haunt us if we're all dead," Nigel retorted.

Freddie swept her light low across the floorboards. The planks shone damply, swelling at the edges, and between two she saw something that her light reflected off of.

Her hand went down faster than her brain could narrate the movement. Her fingers slipped, then closed. She couldn't quite lever it free.

"I need something to pry it loose with," she said over the storm still beating down on them.

"Here," Nigel said, digging a thin, metal pen from his jacket pocket.

She stuck the pen along the floorboards and lifted the item from its resting place.

A bracelet, cracked and softened by time. Two letters stamped into a tiny plate.

D.M.

The floor seemed to tilt, not physically, she knew, but in a deep, cellular way. She saw, with skin-memory clarity, the braided leather on her father's wrist as he lifted her over a puddle outside the shop; the way he'd tap it against the counter while reading, a soft, rhythmic chock; the little gold plate darkening with wear.

Her breath snapped. Something inside her chest made the sound of a torn thread.

"Freddie?" Pru said, immediately nearer, voice changed.

Freddie couldn't speak. She held the bracelet in her palm like a fossil of a long-extinct animal.

Nigel, who had been moving with exaggerated care among the beams, stilled. His face softened at once, and he looked away, not from disinterest but from courtesy, like a man closing a door to a private room.

"There's something else," he said after a moment, and pointed.

In another seam, something else metallic glinted faintly. Freddie reached and pried. A small, old key worked free with effort, flakes of rust falling and scattering in the wind. It was simple, notched, the head flattened by years of being turned by fingers that might have been her father's.

She felt the urge to sit down hard. Instead, she curled the key and bracelet together and stared at them like they might come alive and explain this whole mess to her. The weight in her palm was small yet immense.

And then came the sound she would have known in a hallway full of footsteps: scrape-step, scrape-step, scrape.

The hatch into the stairwell creaked, and a man's silhouette rose out of the hole. The lightning beyond the louvers lit half of his face, then none; she saw the uneven set of his shoulders, the toe-out stance, the left leg that dragged a beat behind the right.

His breath was ragged. When he spoke, the words stumbled out like they'd tripped on a stone.

"I wrote... I wrote it down," he said. The consonants caught as if they were barbed. "He saw me—he... he wasn't s'posed to be there—wasn't—" He swallowed. His gaze cut to Freddie's hand and stuck there, startled by a recognition she couldn't read. "It was an accident," he whispered. "I didn't—"

"Who?" Freddie asked, the word as sharp as a tack. "Who saw you?"

His eyes flared, then skittered. Panic blew through his shape like wind through paper.

"Wait," Nigel said softly, palms lifted. The old actor's instincts slid into his voice—not performance, but that particular gentling cadence you use on a skittish animal. "No one's here to hurt you. Tell us what you wrote."

The man jerked as though someone had tugged a string in his spine, then slammed the hatch and ran.

"Absolutely not," Pru snapped, lunging for the ring to open back the hatch.

It had dropped too far to grab. Nigel's gaze tore across the chamber looking for anything to pry the hatch open and snagged on a relic of a tool left behind for bell maintenance or the like — it was metal and long with a pointed tip. He snatched it up, gave it a once-over, then hooked the iron ring through the pointed end.

"For Queen and country," he grunted, and yanked.

The hatch sprang. They spilled down the spiral, Pru first, then Freddie, then Nigel, the metal tool clattering, their shoulders skimming stone. Lightning crashed so close Freddie felt it in her teeth. Wind shoved down the stairwell with such force that it pushed them onward.

On the last curve, Freddie's heel slipped on wet grit. Nigel's hand closed on the back of her jacket and steadied her, a firm, unshowy grip, then let go quickly when she righted.

"Thanks," she gasped.

"Don't make me do that again," he said, sounding winded and unsure he could be successful a second time.

They burst into the nave and sprinted for the outer doors. The storm hit them as if it had been waiting, driving rain sideways. The limper was already halfway across the churchyard, a lopsided shadow among the stones.

"Left leg," Pru shouted over the weather. "Watch his left. He plants wide before the drag!"

They followed, slipping and pounding, the rain so thick it felt like running through a beaded curtain forever. Headstones rose up like broken teeth, names of past Fernridge rushing at them and away: **Carter. Hern. Smith.** Freddie's light snatched a set of prints—heel-drag, toe-out—then lost them as water pooled and erased.

"By the wall!" Nigel called, pointing to where the cemetery's low stone boundary slumped. The limper sprang, not gracefully, but with the desperate, ugly efficiency of someone who had practiced this escape, and half-tumbled into the thicket beyond. They heard the rush of water a moment later and ran for it, skidding down a short incline slick with algae and moss.

A drainage culvert gaped in the weeds, swallowing a stream of stormwater. Freddie aimed her light into the opening. The beam caught ragged roots and red mud and a swallowed grocery sack. The roar of the culvert made the space vibrate, as if the ground itself were humming.

"Don't you dare," Pru warned, catching Freddie's sleeve. "You are not crawling into a drain where a man who pushes people can also push you."

Freddie's breath sawed. Her light caught something on the edge of the culvert, a smudge of mud with a whisper of tread. Then the next thunder peeled the night clear, and in that brief, obliterating white she thought she saw him glance back from the thicket beyond, face ghost-pale, mouth parted, water streaming off him like a baptism gone wrong. She blinked, then he was gone, the thick brush swallowing sound and shape.

They stood there, drenched to the marrow, and their lungs on fire. Nigel bent forward, palms on his knees, breathing like a man who had just outrun his own past. He laughed once—one stunned, high bark—and then scrubbed a hand over his face.

"That," he managed, "was the most exercise I've had in decades."

Pru made a wet, exasperated noise and clapped him once on the shoulder—hard enough to be corrective, soft enough to be kind. "You did good, Shakespeare."

He tipped his head, rain beading on his lashes. "For what it's worth," he said hoarsely to Freddie, "I think he recognized you, too. The way he looked at your hand when you took the bracelet…I think he knew what it meant."

Freddie pressed her palm harder into her pocket. She was shivering, but not from rain.

They slogged back through the churchyard, past stones that tipped and stones that stood stubbornly straight, past the angel with a broken wing and the lichen-gnawed cross where the grass always grew thin. Freddie kept checking the ground without meaning to, hoping for a print that didn't wash away as she looked at it.

Inside Pru's wagon, the heater wheezed and then found itself. They steamed all the way down Elder Lane. The storm seemed to lose interest as they drove, like a bully finally bored by failing to get a flinch.

Back at the shop, the bell over the door chimed almost politely. The air inside wrapped around them with its old, kind smells: cinnamon, paper, a faint lemon from the wood polish Pru insisted made "the books breathe easier." Aggie stood up on the counter, tail high, and chirruped as if to say *you look terrible—tell me everything.*

Freddie set the bracelet and the key on the counter carefully, as if they might shy and bolt. Aggie lowered his grand head and sniffed the leather once, delicately. His pupils widened. He tapped the bracelet with a paw and then, without fuss, lay down across both objects, chin on the edge, guarding like a dragon with a coin hoard.

"That's our boy," Pru whispered, reaching to stroke his head. Aggie flicked an ear, graciously accepting praise as his due.

Pru fetched towels. Nigel took his with both hands and hid briefly in it, just a man with water in his lashes and not enough breath. When he dropped it, his cheeks were still ruddy, but his expression had gone sober. Shame lived around his mouth the way sudden grief does, soft and surprised.

"Do you—" he began, then stopped. "Forgive me, I— Did he remind you of anyone?"

Freddie met his eyes. "Only of a nightmare."

He nodded, receiving the truth without argument. "He looked at you the way a man looks when he sees a ghost he created," Nigel said quietly. "I've done that once or twice in my life." He made himself smile. It cracked in the middle. "Usually just in rehearsal, mind."

Pru set a steaming mug in front of each of them without asking what they wanted. "I'm going to be bossy," she announced. "We will not go to the drain. We will not call Lila tonight because I do not trust any of us to tell a story that keeps us from getting thrown in protective custody. We will sleep—" her voice softened on the word like it was a spell "—and we will wake up and we will go together. Agreed?"

Freddie almost said no. She looked at the bracelet under Aggie's jaw. **D.M.** She looked at the little key asleep beside it. Every nerve in her wanted to sprint back out into the weather and shake the town until the truth fell out like loose change.

"Agreed," she said, and surprised herself by meaning it.

Freddie found her notebook and did as Father Keating had instructed, she wrote. Her hand didn't shake this time. Block printing each line like she wanted to make a contract with the paper:

A MURDER MOST UNSOLVED

CHURCH TOWER: Bracelet (D.M.). Old key.
Limper in hatch: "I wrote it down…he saw me…accident."
Toe-out, left shoulder dipped.
Vanished toward culvert behind cemetery wall.

She added, in smaller letters: **He recognized the bracelet and me.**

The storm eased its tantrum outside; rain softened to a talk. The spire, briefly lit by an apologetic flash, looked less like a needle now and more like a finger but signaling, not stabbing.

Nigel rose and tugged at his coat as if it might pose better if he coaxed it. "I'll go," he said. "You'll have beds and—I was going to say safety, but I suppose we've all learned not to promise that." His mouth tugged in a rueful line. "If you need me, whistle. I can hear the shop from the theatre on windy nights when it blows just right."

Pru narrowed her eyes. "No more heroic midnight strolls, Nigel."

He pressed a hand to his chest. "God and Rupert Whitcomb being my witnesses."

When he'd gone, the shop seemed to grow taller, somehow. Freddie stood where she was for a long moment, listening to the tired rain. Then she reached and touched Aggie's whiskers with her fingertip. He closed one eye, as if to say: *You're allowed to rest, investigator.*

Freddie didn't sleep so much as stop moving. She dreamed she was climbing a staircase that never arrived anywhere until Winnie stepped out of a landing and said, mildly, *you're on the wrong stairwell, darling. Try the other one.* When she woke, gray had crept into the window and the storm had stepped away to sulk beyond the hills.

The bracelet and the key were still where she'd left them, and Aggie was still there too, chin on the leather, tail a soft question mark.

"You kept watch," she whispered.

He yawned extravagantly, showing all his teeth, then tucked his paws under himself with the air of a cat who has solved everything for everyone.

Freddie reached for her pen again. She underlined one word on last night's page until the paper was impressed.

Key.

Whatever it opened, the lock was somewhere in Fernridge. Somewhere that belonged to a man with a dragging left leg and a story he couldn't say straight. Somewhere that could still tell her what happened the night the world tilted for good.

She closed the notebook and slid it into her pocket. Behind her, the town was starting to wake; the first truck, the first kettle, the first radio low in a kitchen. Fernridge was itself again: human and small and busy with ordinary things.

And Freddie, who had chased a shadow up into a dark tower in a lightning storm, felt the terrible and wonderful truth of it click into place.

They were very close now. Close enough to touch the lock.

Close enough that even a whisper sounded like a confession.

23

THE CHURCH BASEMENT

The heavy oak door of St. Mary's groaned as Freddie pushed it open, a deep sigh that seemed to echo through the nave. The church smelled of rain-soaked stone and trapped rainwater that was quickly growing musty. Her shoes squeaked faintly against the polished floor as she hesitated, clutching her cardboard tray with its two steaming paper coffee cups and the small white paper pastry sack.

Lightning still pulsed beyond the stained glass, throwing fractured patches of jewel-toned light onto the pews. Somewhere higher up, remnants of last night's storm still rattled the louvers in the belfry, as though reminding her where she had been the night before. She swallowed and told herself she wasn't about to turn around and flee back into the storm. Not after what they'd found.

The confessional stood to one side like a dark wooden booth at a fair, its curtain drawn shut. A small light above it glowed softly, as though marking a vacancy sign. Freddie lingered near the closest pew, debating whether to call out Father Keating's name. But something—curiosity, nerves, maybe the faintest glimmer of mischief—nudged her forward. If she wanted his attention, well...she knew where to find him.

She slid the curtain aside. Inside, the confessional was a small, warm space, polished, but a little worn. Her hand hovered over the seat before she sat gingerly, tucking her tray against her lap. A tiny grille separated her from the opposite side, where she could just make out a figure shifting slightly.

For a heartbeat she almost bolted. But instead she leaned forward, cleared her throat, and whispered the opening line she'd seen in movies, "Father, forgive me. It has been, well... I've never actually been to confession. Mostly because I'm not actually Catholic, though I'm not opposed to becoming but that's not why I'm here this morning."

There was a long pause. Then, to her surprise, Father Keating laughed—a warm, genuine laugh that filled the narrow booth. "Well now, that's a first. The non-Catholics don't usually try the furniture out in the confessional." He tapped lightly on the wood. "Come on out, Miss March. We'll both suffocate in here if you stay. Though we can work on converting you later." She could hear the smile in his voice.

She slipped back through the curtain and emerged, a little sheepish. Father Keating stepped out on his side, straightening his clerical collar. Freddie noticed for the first time that he was a pleasant looking man, attractive certainly. His features were kind but lined from years of hearing stories, good and bad. His eyes twinkled when they landed on the cardboard tray.

Freddie held it up like an offering. "Peace offering or bribe. Take your pick. Coffee, and chocolate chip scones from Pru's."

His brows lifted. "Blessed are the bribers, for they shall inherit my gratitude." He reached for the cup, then tapped the sack. "Next time, though—chocolate chocolate chip. That's the true path to sainthood, especially for non-Catholics."

She smiled despite herself and her *only* half-successful bribe. "Duly noted."

They moved to a pew, the storm a steady percussion behind the walls. Father Keating lowered himself onto the worn wood with the sigh of someone who had spent decades carrying both bodies and souls. Freddie sat beside him, setting her cup on the bench between them. For a moment, she felt almost like a little girl again, with Winnie holding her hand in the same pew during Christmas Eve services. Only this time, Winnie was gone, and the weight of what Freddie carried pressed against her shoulders like an anchor.

She told him everything—the hidden notes from Winnie's investigation, the night someone broke into the bookstore, that they'd been in the bell tower and found a bracelet and a key, the limper with his broken sentences. How Nigel had hauled open the hatch with an metal rod and how they had chased a shadow through rain-slicked graves. She even told him about the Motor Court and even went back as far as to tell him about her reluctance to come back to Fernridge and her guilt about all the lost years with Winnie. Her words tumbled, awkward at first, then faster, desperate for someone steady enough to absorb them.

If Father Keating was shocked, he didn't show it. His expression remained calm, stone-like, his eyes intent. Only occasionally did he sip his coffee, nodding gently, as though she were recounting nothing more unusual than a quarrel with a neighbor. He'd spent decades listening to confessions—this much she realized—hearing the worst of people in whispers. A bracelet and a stuttered half-confession weren't going to knock him flat.

When she finished, she felt hollowed out. Her coffee and scone had gone untouched.

"I don't know what to do next," she admitted, her voice low. "I don't even know if I should have told you."

Father Keating turned his coffee cup between his hands, his gaze on the far altar where candles flickered. "You should tell Deputy Barrett," he said. His tone carried no hesitation, only practical certainty. "In fact, I'm surprised you haven't already."

Freddie winced. "Yes. Pru and Nigel made me promise. We're planning to go see her later this morning. But before that…you mentioned something once. The church bulletins. You said I could look through them. Just in case. I wondered if I could—before I talk to the deputy. Maybe there's something there."

The priest considered this, his lips pursed. Then he nodded. "All right. But I'll be there with you." He rose, setting his empty cup on the pew arm. "Can't have parishioners wandering into the basement without supervision. Insurance nightmare." His mouth quirked. "Besides, I'd like to see what you're looking for."

He walked to the confessional, scribbled something on a scrap of paper, and taped it neatly to the door. In bold block letters: *Back in 30 minutes. Say your prayers until then.* Freddie smothered a laugh, following him down the side aisle toward the stairs.

The basement was cooler, a faint smell of mildew under the detergent tang from the parish laundry. Fluorescent tubes flickered overhead. Father Keating led her to a corner lined with metal shelves, where boxes were stacked in tidy rows. He stooped, grunted, and hauled out a long cardboard file box, setting it on a folding table.

"Old bulletins," he said, brushing dust from his hands. "Every bake sale, every choir schedule, every plea for volunteers since I first set foot here. My secret weapon when I need to guilt someone into leading the Easter pageant."

Freddie opened the lid, the cardboard whispering. Inside were file folders, each labeled with a year. She slid out the stack for the late nineties, the years Father Keating had mentioned when the bell tower needed repair and also the time when her own father had disappeared. The bulletins were folded sheets, each dated neatly.

She began flipping through them. At first, it was small-town minutiae—reminders for Bible study, potluck suppers, choir rehearsals. A bulletin from June featured a picture of a summer fair, with booths strung along Main Street. She paused at one, her breath catching.

There she was. Seven-ish years old, front teeth missing, grinning up at the camera while holding a plate of cookies beside Winnie. Her grandmother's hand was on her shoulder. In the background, Pru stood behind a table loaded with pies, her hair in a long braid that weaved down to her waist. Freddie traced the photo with her thumb, a lump tightening in her throat.

She kept turning pages. Announcements blurred by: youth group car washes, harvest festivals, pancake breakfasts. Then—finally—something different. A bulletin dated late October. Across the top, in bold, Fundraiser for Bell Tower Repairs. Below, an article explained that the bell mechanism had suffered water damage and needed significant work. The parish would host a bean and chili supper to raise money.

Freddie leaned closer. But the bottom half of the page was gone, torn jaggedly away. Worse, when she flipped to the next folder, the following months of bulletins weren't there. November and December were both gone. She picked up the following year's folder and found that January was missing also. The folder picked up again the following spring as if nothing had happened.

She glanced up. Father Keating's brow furrowed as he leaned over her shoulder. He rifled through the folder, checked the box, even searched the shelf for a stray stack. Nothing.

"That's strange," he said finally, rubbing his jaw. "I've kept these in order for years. Never had a gap."

"Could someone have taken them?" Freddie asked. Her voice felt small in the humming basement.

He hesitated. "Possibly. But who would want church bulletins from twenty-odd years ago?" He looked at her, eyes thoughtful. "Unless those bulletins held something someone didn't want remembered."

Freddie touched the torn edge again. Her stomach knotted. Whatever had been on the missing half, whatever had followed in the missing months, was exactly what she needed. And someone had known that.

Father Keating stayed bent over the box for a while, flipping folders with the deliberate care of a man turning pages in someone else's diary. Then he closed the lid and leaned his hip against the table, studying Freddie's face.

"You know," he said, voice softening, "I didn't know your grandmother for who she truly was until a rummage sale about twenty-five years ago. We were drowning in other people's treasures and our own foolishness. Someone donated an entire set of encyclopedias missing the letter M, which, in a town that survives on muffins and magnolias and melodrama, felt like a hate crime. I was fretting about how to price it." He smiled. "Winnie took a grease pencil, wrote 'A–Z, Minus Misadventures,' slapped a dollar on it, and it sold in five minutes to a boy who only wanted the letter J because he liked jaguars."

Freddie's laugh came out a little wobbly. "That sounds like her."

"She was kind," he said. "But she didn't confuse kindness with being nice. She told the truth the way a good seamstress cuts cloth, with confidence, and a plan to mend it if she cut it wrong." His gaze drifted toward the ceiling. "I admired that."

He was quiet a moment. When he spoke again, the timbre changed, lighter, and at the same time more careful. "I knew your father, too."

Freddie's hand tightened on the torn bulletin. The basement light hummed audibly, as if leaning in.

"Not from the confessional," he added immediately, a quick glance her way as if to head off the worry that he might be about to trespass on sacred ground. "I can't and won't ever share what belongs to God. I mean ordinary parish things. Daniel came to youth nights sometimes—half there for the pizza, half there to argue with me about whether Saint Augustine would have enjoyed baseball."

"Would he?" Freddie asked, before she could stop herself.

"I like to think so," Father Keating said, smiling. "He loved order, and what is a strike zone if not a little square of theology?" The smile faded to something more reflective. "Daniel could be a live wire. Quick to laugh. Quick to leave when the room felt too small." He nodded toward the nave above them. "One spring, he came to help me repair the hymnals. The spines were splitting; our music was molting. I'll never forget, he took to the work like it mattered, lined each binding up, pressed cloth into glue with such care you'd think we were patching a sail in a storm. He wore a bracelet then, leather that he had stamped himself at the county fair, he told me. D.M. with a little dot between."

A small, involuntary sound escaped Freddie—half intake of breath, half soft ache. "The bracelet we found last night," she murmured. "Leather. Stamped D.M. It was wedged into a crack by the ladder up there."

He nodded once, slowly. "Then at least one piece of the past is where you think it is." He glanced down at the torn bulletin again. "As for the other pieces, someone doesn't want us finding them."

Freddie brushed the ragged edge with her thumb. "Do you think it was him? The man from the tower last night?" She swallowed the name, feeling suddenly superstitious about speaking it in a church basement. "The limping man. He said, 'I wrote it down…he saw me…it was an accident.' If the bracelet was Daniel's then 'he' is…"

Father Keating let her finish the thought in the privacy of her own mind. "What a terrible knot grief makes when it tangles with guilt," he said at last. "Two lines that never meant to cross, and yet…" He opened his hands. "Here we are."

A sound, faint and out of place, snicked across the concrete hall outside the storage area. Freddie's head jerked up. Father Keating's eyes sharpened.

"What was—" she began.

He lifted a palm, listening. The fluorescent light above them hummed on, but another bulb near the door shivered and went dark, then sputtered back to life with a thin, metallic ping. Somewhere beyond the rows of metal shelves, a door settled into its frame with a careful click—too careful, like fingers guiding it closed to avoid the natural slam.

They stood in the same instant, without discussing it, the old priest surprisingly light on his feet, his hand making a small, calming motion that said both to stay near and not to be afraid. He reached for the pegboard by the stairs and unhooked a flashlight, thumbing it on. The beam made a pale tunnel through the dust.

They moved together down the narrow corridor, past a steel sink and a box of wax votive stubs marked TO MELT, past the closet where defunct nativity sheep leaned with lopsided devotion against a broken folding manger. The air was cooler here and carried a faint mineral smell, as if the church's foundation still remembered being earth.

Another sound—scuff, pause, retreat—breathed from the hall that led to the side stairs. Father Keating angled the light. The concrete held a few distinct footprints in a shallow film of dust tracked down from the stairs after last night's storm: heel, toe, heel, toe... and a subtle outward splay on the left. Not much. Just enough for Freddie's chest to clamp around her heart.

"Toe-out," she whispered before she could stop herself.

Father Keating's beam slid to the side door. The push bar was flush, the lock thrown. But the metal around the strike plate was freshly scarred, a faint crescent where a tool had marred it. A draft threaded under the door, carrying with it the clean smell of rain-damp grass.

"Was this locked?" Freddie asked.

"It will be now," he said. His voice was calm enough to be mistaken for casual. He checked the bar again, then deliberately flipped the extra deadbolt. Only then did he angle the light back down to the floor.

Near the baseboard, just where the door met the slab, a tiny curl of paper had caught on a splinter. He crouched with more ease than his knees liked and teased it free, passing the beam to Freddie so he could squint at the scrap. It was little more than a comma of newsprint. But when he flipped it over, one word—half a word, really—could still be made out in ghosted ink: **...light**.

Not proof. Not even a breadcrumb. A speck, and yet.

The overhead light buzzed again, complaining. The priest rose, slipped the scrap into his pocket, and glanced at Freddie. "Let's not turn this into a ghost story," he said gently. "Whoever it was, is gone. But we were right not allowing you to come down here alone."

They retraced their steps to the table. For a while they worked in companionable silence—Freddie checking folder pockets just in case someone had misfiled November into April, Father Keating making tidy notes on a yellow legal pad: **Missing: bulletins Nov–Jan, 1998–99. Torn page Oct.** When they had exhausted the box, and the small hope of miracles, he set the legal pad down and laced his fingers.

"I'm going to call Lila," he said. "Not because you can't. Because I promised your grandmother once I'd do the right thing if her girl asked me for help." He angled a look at Freddie that was both kind and firm. "And because someone slid a tool into my church door."

Freddie nodded. "I told you we'd go," she said. "We will." Then, the question she hadn't realized she needed to ask until it stood at the edge of her tongue: "Father—do you think I'm wrong? To keep pulling at this?"

He didn't answer immediately. He took off his glasses, wiped them with the handkerchief priests always seem to have, and put them back on as if he wanted to see her clearly when he spoke. "I think the reason matters," he said. "If you're pulling because the thread frightens you and you want it gone, you'll tear the sweater. If you're pulling because something is strangling the town and you mean to loosen it, you'll save someone's breath."

She swallowed. "I keep thinking—if I stop, I'm leaving her twice."

"Then don't stop," he said simply. "But don't do it alone, either. Solitude might sharpen the mind and speed things along but it erodes the heart." His mouth tilted. "That last line is from my own private book of proverbs. Winnie would have edited it for style."

"She would have added a comma," Freddie said, surprising herself with a small laugh.

"She would have added a pie," Father Keating countered. He checked his watch, then glanced toward the confessional sign upstairs as if he could see it through the floor. "I need to be back to my booth or half the town will think I've run away with the choir fund. Can you spare two more minutes so I can show you one last thing?"

He ducked behind the rows of shelving to a low cabinet with a warped door and tugged it open. Inside, a jumble of parish leftovers—old candle snuffers, a cracked processional cross, a coil of twine—spilled like props from a poorly organized pageant. From behind the twine he drew out a flat archival envelope and set it on the table with a certain ceremonial care.

"Every priest has a box where he keeps things he doesn't know what to do with," he said. "Sometimes that box is metaphorical. Mine is literal. This is from the spring after the bell repairs. It was tucked into the music stand in the choir loft. No note. No signature."

He eased the flap and slid out a single sheet of yellowed paper. The top was blank, save for the church letterhead—ST. MARY'S,

FERNRIDGE—faded to a ghost of itself. Below, a few lines typed on an old machine:

The bells are fixed but wrong.
The sound is right but not honest.
I was there. I should tell.
I don't know how to tell without breaking everything.

Under that, in shaky pen, someone had written: *Forgive me.*

Freddie stared at the page, an electric prickle moving up her arms. "Why do you have this?"

"Because there are two kinds of notes a parish receives," he said quietly. "One kind belongs to the suggestion box. The other kind belongs to the mercy of God. I didn't know which kind this was." He slid the envelope back toward her. "You can take a photograph of it. I can't hand you the original. But I think this is the voice of your limping man—or someone very like him. The typewriter we had in the office then had a sticky 'R.' See how the tops of these Rs are faint? The choir director sometimes used the machine to type programs. The paper came from our cabinet. Whoever wrote this was here."

Freddie snapped a photo on her phone, then one more in case her hands had shaken. The words sat harshly on her screen. *The sound is right but not honest.* She thought of the bell's placid face against storm clouds. She thought of Daniel's bracelet pressed into a crack like a swallowed cry. She breathed out slowly through her nose to keep from making a sound in a room that belonged to God.

When she looked up, Father Keating was watching her with a kind of sturdy compassion that didn't pity and didn't flinch. "You don't have to be strong every minute," he said.

"I know," she said, and found that she did really know.

They put the folders back into the box together. He taped the lid shut with a bright strip of blue painter's tape.

The climb back to the nave felt longer than the descent had, but brighter. The candles guttered on the altar and then steadied. Rain pawed lightly at the stained-glass saints like a polite visitor asking to be let in.

At the top of the stairs, the confessional's tiny light still glowed. Father Keating plucked his scrap sign from the door and folded it into his pocket. Then he turned to her, hesitation and mischief wrestling briefly across his face before mischief won.

"One last pastoral abuse of my office," he said. "If you plan to tell Lila today—and you should—let me call first to tell her about the bulletins. I could even ask her to meet you here, in the sanctuary, instead of at the station if you'd like. People tell the truth more easily in rooms that remember them kindly."

"You make it sound like the pews keep score," Freddie said.

"They do," he replied. "But only of who needs a cushion." He grew sober again. "Freddie—if this gets heavier than you can carry, say so. I am old enough to have learned the difference between martyrdom and foolishness."

"Winnie would say martyrdom doesn't go with my complexion," she said, the joke arriving of its own accord, which felt like a mercy.

He inclined his head. "Winnie would say a great many things. Most of them funny, and the rest true." He tipped his chin toward the doors. "Go on now. Pru will worry if you're late. And Aggie," he smiled, "Aggie will judge."

"Thanks for offering your pews as a witness stand, but I think we'll just go visit Deputy Barrett at the station. I think I'll be more open away from the location of last night's excitement. Not to mention, I don't think we'll have any unwanted visitors eavesdropping from the shadows around all the town's police."

He nodded in agreement then took two steps toward the booth, but paused. "Oh, and Miss March?"

She turned.

"If you find yourself up in that tower again, call me first to hold the ladder."

"I will," she said, and meant it.

They parted there—the priest to his booth, where small towns bring both sins and forgiveness, and Freddie to the wet brightness beyond the doors. As she pushed the heavy oak open, she glanced back once.

She would go to Pru. Then to Deputy Barrett. Then, whatever came next.

Behind her, a single bell struck the hour. The sound was right. Whether it was honest, well, that was why she was here.

24

THE NAME IN THE FILE

The fluorescent lights in Deputy Barrett's office buzzed with the faintest hum, like hornets trapped in glass. Freddie sat on the edge of the hard plastic chair opposite Deputy Barrett's desk, twisting her fingers together until they went white. Pru lounged beside her with the deceptive calm of someone who could spring into fiery defense at the first whiff of bad news. Nigel had insisted on tagging along. He was perched against the filing cabinet with his arms crossed, looking as if he were about to give a soliloquy on justice, fate, and their innocence.

Deputy Barrett closed a manila folder, rested her hands on top of it, and regarded the three of them over the rim of her glasses. She didn't speak right away. The silence prickled across Freddie's skin like static.

Finally, Deputy Barrett leaned back. "I've sent the bracelet to the state lab," she said, voice steady. "DNA testing takes time, though, so we won't have results back for weeks. But I don't want you thinking nothing's happening."

Freddie nodded, though her pulse rattled in her ears. She had carried that bracelet in her pocket for a whole night and a partial day before surrendering it, fingers brushing against the worn leather as if it could tether her father back home. She couldn't wait until the bracelet was sent back to her. Deputy Barrett had promised her once it was no longer needed, she'd return it to her. Freddie longed for this mess to finally be over and all the mystery surrounding her loved ones to be resolved.

Deputy Barrett tapped the folder with a blunt fingertip. "While we wait, I've been digging." She glanced at Freddie, then at Nigel, then back again. "You said the tower. 1998. A bracelet with initials D.M. That gave me a starting point."

"Please tell me it's more than initials and bad memories," Pru said, folding her arms.

Deputy Barrett's expression softened for half a breath. "Hospital intake logs," she said. "St. Mary's only had one set of records from that season that stood out. An alias, E. Pike. Showed up in the ER after what they called a 'fall near the tower.' Limping, cuts on his hands, possible concussion."

Freddie's breath stalled.

"On the intake sheet, the name is Pike," Deputy Barrett went on. "But one of the EMTs scribbled a note in the margin. Said the man mumbled his real name through the morphine haze before he backtracked. That name was Silas Crowley."

The office shrank around the sound of it. *Silas Crowley*. A name to pin to the limping shadow that had haunted the edges of every story.

Freddie whispered it aloud. "Silas Crowley." The syllables tasted like iron.

Deputy Barrett nodded once. "I pulled everything I could find. In 1998, he worked for a construction company that was in town doing work on the church bell tower and the town stoplight. After 1999, his trail goes cold. No driver's license renewals. No property in his name. He's the kind who drifts with cash work, cheap motels, maybe hiding in plain sight when he has to. But in a town this size?" She shook her head. "He didn't drift far."

Nigel cleared his throat, shifting against the filing cabinet. "Crowley," he said, as though rehearsing. "It has the weight of a villain. Dickens would've loved it."

"No one's writing novels here," Deputy Barrett snapped. Then, after a pause, she softened her tone. "But maybe someone wrote letters."

Freddie's hands trembled in her lap. *Silas.* The limper. The one who had said *I wrote it down... it was an accident.* He had a name. And somehow that made him more dangerous than ever.

Deputy Barrett slid a stack of photocopied pages across the desk. "Freddie, you asked me once if small things matter. They do. I started checking old police blotters, petty crime reports, stuff that never made it far in investigating."

Freddie pulled the pages closer. Grainy print and faded ink scrolled down the columns: **Donation Box Theft at St. Mary's**, **Loose Change Missing from Bakery Jar**, **Antique Prayer Book Vanishes at Rummage Sale.**

"They look random," Deputy Barrett said. "But they're not. These happened in a neat pattern, every few weeks in '98. Low-level thefts, coins, small antiques, enough to make people annoyed but not suspicious. Escalated, though."

Freddie traced the dates with her finger. *June. July. August.* And then—

"They stop," she murmured.

Deputy Barrett nodded. "Abruptly. The last one's September first. After that, nothing. That's the week Daniel, your dad, disappeared."

The storm clouds of realization rolled low in Freddie's chest. Winnie had always said Daniel's vanishing was the moment Fernridge changed, when suspicion and whispers rooted deeper than magnolias. Now, these thefts painted a different picture. Not a ghost story. A man. Silas Crowley.

"He panicked," Pru said suddenly, voice sharper than usual. "He was stealing little bits, got caught—or almost caught. Daniel saw him. And then—"

"Fatal struggle," Deputy Barrett finished, steady but grim. "That's my theory."

The room held its breath.

Nigel, unable to stand the quiet, clapped his hands softly against his knees. "Of course, one can't overlook the alternative theories. Gossip travels faster than truth, as I've learned. Some of the old-timers in town still swear Daniel had gambling debts."

Freddie's head snapped toward him. "That's not true."

"I didn't say I believed it either," Nigel said, holding his palms up. "But you should know what others may say. To their minds, a young man vanishes, leaves a note behind. It's easier to believe he ran off chasing cards than..." He gestured vaguely. "...than murder among the magnolias."

Pru glared at him. "Magnolias don't kill people. People kill people."

Nigel winced. "Yes, yes, point taken. I didn't mean..." His last thought went unspoken as he gave up on that secondary line of accusations.

Deputy Barrett leaned forward, her scowl tempered with patience. "Daniel March had no debt record. No IOUs. No criminal file. Don't let anyone plant that seed in your head, Freddie. False trails waste more than time, they break families twice."

Freddie felt her throat tighten. "Thank you," she whispered.

Deputy Barrett gave her a short nod, then gathered the folder back. "This is where we stand. Silas Crowley's our name. His thefts fit the pattern. The bracelet ties to your father. But none of this is courtroom-ready."

The meeting broke after that, though Freddie's mind spun like a wheel that refused to slow. Outside the sheriff's office, the summer heat pressed heavily against her skin, and the air was so humid her lungs fought for extra breath.

Pru hooked her arm through Freddie's. "You okay?"

"No," Freddie said honestly. "But I feel... clearer. Like we've been chasing smoke and now I can finally see the fire."

Nigel trailed behind them, uncharacteristically subdued. "I must admit," he said, voice rough, "the story grows darker by the chapter. Poor Winnie knew something was festering, and it cost her."

Freddie swallowed hard. "Then I won't stop until I know exactly what."

They walked past the square where townsfolk milled in the heat—someone selling peaches out of a truck bed, children skipping rope. The normalcy clashed painfully with the storm of names and dates in Freddie's mind.

She clutched her notebook to her chest like armor. Tonight, she would write it all down: *Silas Crowley is E. Pike. Theft pattern. 1998.* No more shadows without names.

And as the lantern light from the shop windows spilled out across Fernridge's quiet street, the truth felt one step closer, sharp and unyielding as the edge of a blade.

That evening, back at The Marple & Quill, Aggie sprawled across the counter like a bloated sentry. Freddie laid the photocopies down beside him. The cat sniffed them, then draped a paw across the page marked **Antique Prayer Book Vanishes.**

"Guard it, Aggie," Freddie murmured, scratching behind his ears. "Guard it like treasure."

The bell above the shop door jingled, and for a wild second, Freddie imagined Silas himself standing there. But it was someone Freddie was happy to see, Father Keating, ducking in with a smile and a paper bag of still-warm rolls.

"You look like you've seen a ghost," he said gently but his eyebrows furrowed in concern.

"Not a ghost actually," Freddie replied, her voice low and certain. Father Keating set the bag of rolls down on the counter, then accepted the cup of tea Freddie poured for him. He got comfortable in the chair near the front window, where the evening light streaked across the floorboards in gold slants. For a few minutes, they just talked about nothing, how the roses outside St. Mary's had taken well to the rain, how Aggie had nearly stolen half a scone from the church bake sale table. They were preparing for the deeper conversation to come.

Then Freddie leaned forward, lowering her voice. "Deputy Barrett told me the name. Silas Crowley. She showed me the thefts, the trail, everything. It's all tied to that summer in '98. But after September 1st, the trail runs cold, and that's exactly when my dad went missing."

Father Keating's lined face grew thoughtful. "Ah." He folded his hands, and for a long moment he looked at them, as though searching for the right words in the map of veins across his skin. Then he said, quietly, "You know, there was something else that happened right about September first, 1998. Something I hadn't thought about until now."

Freddie's pulse jumped. "What?"

"My church secretary, Lynette McCloud, died." His voice softened, almost reverent. "At the time, everyone said it was old age that carried her off. She was only in her sixties, but she kept herself spry. She lived in the stone cottage right next to the church tower. I remember thinking, even then, how strange it was, her passing so suddenly. And now, all this...it seems too much of a coincidence."

Freddie's breath caught. "Do you think she saw something she shouldn't have? Like my dad did?"

Father Keating's eyes met hers. "It is possible. Perhaps she knew, or perhaps she heard something from that cottage window. And if so...maybe she paid for it."

The thought made Freddie's stomach churn. Two deaths. Two lives were silenced to cover someone's tracks. "Her death, her funeral...those would've been published in the church bulletins."

"Yes," Father Keating said, brow furrowing again. "In fact, I remember writing her tribute myself. A lengthy one, full of her devotion to the church, her years of service. And those would have appeared in the very bulletins missing from the file box. Conveniently missing, you might say."

Freddie swallowed. "We need to tell Deputy Barrett."

Father Keating nodded. "We do."

They called Deputy Barrett, who agreed to meet them at the shop.

Then he added, almost apologetically, "I've kept journals since seminary. Daily notes, really…just scraps about sermons, parishioners, the little comings and goings of life. But I know I wrote about Lynette's death in detail, I was the one who discovered her body and it was quite a shock to me. I can fetch it, see if there's more that I've forgotten."

"Do it," Freddie said firmly.

Father Keating rose, brushing the crumbs from his lap. "I'll be back shortly." He tipped his head in farewell and slipped out into the cooling evening.

By the time the deputy pushed through the door, twilight had thickened, and the lanterns in the bookstore windows had begun to glow.

"Good evening," Deputy Barrett said as she stepped inside, greeted by the waiting cup of tea and a lemon bar on a plate. Her eyebrows lifted in genuine surprise. "You and Pru always know how to make a girl feel welcome."

"Of course we do," Freddie replied warmly, sliding the plate closer to her. "Winnie wouldn't have it any other way."

Deputy Barrett picked up the lemon bar and took a generous bite, closing her eyes for a beat. "Mercy," she muttered around a mouthful. "If you two ever decide to give up on books, you could run this whole town on baked goods alone."

Freddie laughed softly. "That's mostly Pru. She thinks pastry is the best form of persuasion. And honestly, she's not wrong."

Deputy Barrett gave a small huff that might have been a laugh if she weren't so tired, then glanced around the shop. "Where's Father Keating?"

"He ran back over to the church," Freddie said, watching the deputy settle in. "Wanted to dig out his old journal, he's sure he wrote something down about that time. I think he remembers less than he wishes he did."

Deputy Barrett nodded, more focused on the steaming tea than the explanation, her fingers wrapped tightly around the mug. For once, some of her edges seemed to soften. In the lamplight of the bookshop, with a plate of sweets in front of her, she looked less like the unshakable deputy and more like any other weary neighbor trying to catch her breath after too much bad news.

Freddie noticed the small shift and felt something tighten in her chest—gratitude, maybe, or simply the strange comfort of knowing that even the strongest people still needed their lemon bars and a quiet corner to lean on.

Freddie and Deputy Barrett sat in the shop together, the silence stretching. Finally, Deputy Barrett said, "You've been carrying a lot for someone your age."

Freddie gave a shaky laugh. "Tomorrow's my birthday, actually."

Deputy Barrett blinked. "And you didn't tell anyone?"

"What's there to celebrate? With everything going on, it feels selfish. Wrong."

The deputy's gaze softened, a rare flicker of warmth breaking through her usual armor. "Freddie, with all this death and mayhem swirling around you, now is exactly the time to celebrate. Another year means you're still here. It means you've got a chance to keep going, to keep fighting."

Freddie hesitated, then let out a breath that turned into laughter. "Maybe you're right."

"Of course I'm right," Deputy Barrett said, cracking the faintest smile. "And if you don't tell Pru, I will and then she'll throw confetti in your tea."

They were still laughing when the bell above the door jingled again. Father Keating staggered inside, one hand clamped to his forehead. Blood ran down his temple, dripping onto his clerical collar.

Freddie leapt up. "Father!"

He swayed, his face pale. In his other hand was nothing—not the journal he had promised to retrieve. "Someone...someone hit me," he gasped. "Took the journal. They knew...they knew I had it."

Then his knees buckled, and he collapsed to the floor.

"I'll call an ambulance!" Deputy Barrett yelled, pulling her phone from her pocket.

Freddie dropped beside him, pressing her hands against the bandage he held, her heart hammering. Aggie yowled from the counter, tail lashing, as though the cat himself knew the shadows had struck again.

The sirens were already wailing in the distance by the time Father Keating's eyes fluttered shut.

25

A Knock on the Head

The hospital had that scrubbed-clean smell that tried and failed to cover the metallic undertone of worry. Fluorescent lights hummed above a corridor of beige curtains and laminated posters about handwashing and fall prevention. A volunteer in a pink vest rolled past with a cart of magazines no one wanted to read. Somewhere, a monitor kept a steady, reassuring beep-beep-beep.

Father Keating looked very human in a hospital bed.

They'd propped him half-upright, a square of white gauze taped at his hairline where blood had matted his silver hair. The gown did unflattering things to his dignity, but his eyes were clear, if a little glassy with pain meds. When Freddie stepped into the room with Pru, Nigel, and Deputy Barrett at her shoulder, he tried to sit taller, winced, and settled for smoothing the blanket instead.

"Well," he said, voice hoarse but warm, "if this is the welcoming committee, then I must be more important than I realized."

"Don't flatter yourself," Pru sniffed, though her hand lingered on the bed rail longer than necessary. "We just came to make sure you hadn't driven the nurses mad yet."

Father Keating chuckled, then winced, pressing a hand gingerly to his temple. "Head still feels like someone rang the church bell from inside my skull."

Freddie eased into the chair at his side, her chest tight. "Do you... remember anything? Who hit you?"

He rubbed his temple with the heel of his hand. "I remember making a poor decision to come back alone and fetch the journal, thinking, 'This is foolish, Jeremiah,' and doing it anyway. Then, a footstep behind me that I mistook for the building settling. Pain like lightning. The floor up and met me. When I woke, the journal was gone." He let out a breath that trembled once, then steadied. "Whatever I knew then, I don't... quite... now."

Freddie's mouth flattened, fury and worry braided tight. "I never should've let you go back alone. What was I thinking?"

He held up a hand. "You warned me to be careful. I did a poor job complying. I apologize to the lot of you and to my skull."

Nigel hovered near the curtain, unusually subdued. "You gave us a fright, Father."

"I gave myself one, too," Father Keating admitted. "But before I left the church, I'd skimmed that old entry from the day Lynette died. It's not as good an entry as I hoped." His eyes flicked to Freddie, then Deputy Barrett. "I'd made a joke I shouldn't have. The ladies' choir wanted to meet about hymnals—God save us from committees about committees—and Lynette was late. I said something like 'Perhaps she's decided death would be preferable to this meeting,' which got a cheap laugh." He closed his eyes briefly. "Then I went to check on her. The cottage door was ajar. She was in her chair with a book open in her lap. Cup of tea on the side table, half-drunk, gone cold."

Freddie sucked in air so fast it hurt. The room seemed to tilt. "That's exactly how I found Winnie," she whispered.

Deputy Barrett didn't blink. "Crowley," she said flatly, as if placing a chess piece with the surety of a check. "He did it then, and he did it now."

Father Keating's brow furrowed. "You're certain?"

"I tested Winnie's teacup and it came back positive for poison," Deputy Barrett said, gaze never leaving the priest. "Winifred March had digitalis in her system. Foxglove. Easy enough to find in a cottage garden. It fits a pattern—peaceful staging, tea, a book. Lynette McCloud in '98. Now Winnie."

Pru covered her mouth with her hand. Her eyes shone and she shook her head, sharply, like a person refusing a reality she nevertheless believed. Nigel exhaled the word on a sigh—"Goodness"—and leaned back against the wall, as if to keep his legs from giving out.

Father Keating closed his eyes, not to hide but to hold the moment still. "Then my bad joke will be with me a long time," he said quietly. "I'm sorry, Lynette."

A nurse swept in with professional briskness, checked vitals, and glanced at the cluster. "Five more minutes," she warned gently, "then Father Keating needs to rest. Concussions aren't all created equal."

"We'll be quick," Deputy Barrett said, turning back to the bed. "Father, did you ever note anything in that journal about people hanging around the bell tower back then? Strangers? The bell construction crew showing too much interest in the rest of the church?"

"Bits and pieces," he said. "Names of those who donated to the fix, who to thank at Sunday announcements. A quip from one of the men about the ladder being a death trap. I remember writing down that we'd done the blessing on the new mechanism the same week the stoplight went in on Main." He grimaced. "Now the one thing I most need is the one thing taken."

Deputy Barrett's jaw worked. "I spent half the night digging, too. We had a flood in the station basement about ten years ago. I could cheerfully set fire to the pipes in that building. Most of the old paper records are pulp. I found a brief sheet on Lynette: 'No signs of forced entry. Natural causes presumed. Age-related.' That was that." She shook her head. "It never should've been that."

"People believe what feels safest," Father Keating murmured. "I'm not sure I blame them. I'd wanted to believe it, too."

Freddie laid her hand on the bedrail. "Why take your journal, though? If Crowley only wanted to scare us, he could've hit you and run. He wanted whatever you wrote."

"Which means he thinks there's something incriminating in there," Deputy Barrett said. "Or something that connects him to Lynette's death, or Daniel's disappearance. Or he didn't have a clue what he was taking from the Father and just took it in case we were on to something, just covering all his bases."

Nigel, pale beneath the hospital lights, found a shred of his old theatricality. "It means he's watching," he said. "He knew the moment you decided to fetch it, Father."

Deputy Barrett's gaze snapped to him, then to Freddie and Pru. "This is the part where I repeat myself: He's surveilling you. Maybe not in a grand, cinematic way—maybe it's just a pair of eyes from a parked car. Maybe it's a neighbor's porch. But he is." She breathed out through her nose, slow. "I need you to change your patterns. Don't walk alone at night. If you get a hunch to go somewhere, text me first. Don't post plans. Don't trust 'friendly' notes."

Freddie nodded. "We will."

The nurse returned with a practiced smile and a plastic cup of pills. "Time's up, folks. He needs to sleep if he's going to keep delivering homilies that make you cry."

"They're not that bad," Father Keating protested mildly.

"They're very good," the nurse countered, and tucked the sheet around him with competence that bordered on affection. "Out we go."

They filed into the corridor with small waves and words of "get well soon." The door snicked shut behind them, leaving the beeping and the linen smell to do their quiet work.

In the elevator lobby, Pru pressed her palms to her eyes and took two steadying breaths. "I hate this," she said into her hands. "I hate that he's hurt and that Lynette—Winnie—" Her voice snagged.

Freddie looped an arm around her shoulders and squeezed. Nigel stared at the terrazzo floor like it might have answers in the flecks. Deputy Barrett watched the doors, the hall, the small cluster of people waiting, all at once.

"What now?" Freddie asked.

"Now we get real boring and real careful," Deputy Barrett said. "And we keep working. I'll put out feelers with any pawn shops within a fifty-mile radius for a stuttering man with a limp just in case he's stealing and pawning things to survive. We might be able to catch him if he's frequenting certain shops." She rubbed her temple. "And I want prints from the church hallway, though a thousand hands have touched that banister. I'll try anyway."

"The bell tower stairwell might hold some fingerprints of interest as well, not to include our prints," Nigel added with a head nod to Pru and Freddie.

The elevator dinged. They crowded inside, the metal walls reflecting their worried faces back at them. Nigel, desperate for levity, murmured, "He-who-shall-not-be-named is upping the stakes, then."

"Don't," Freddie said sharply, and immediately softened. "Sorry. I just—I don't want to make him a legend in our mouths."

"Quite right," Nigel said, chastened. "No nicknames, then. Only his end."

They spilled into the humid afternoon, the hospital's automatic doors exhaling them into heat and summer haze. Water glittered in the parking lot potholes from a brief noon shower. Somewhere near, a cicada wound up like a tiny motor.

Nigel offered a half-bow toward Freddie. "I'll go check on Rupert and make sure the theatre has its ladders chained to the floor. Also, I suppose I'll scrounge for tea. A man must keep up morale." He glanced at Pru. "We'll do something kinder for the Father when he's home, yes? A ham? A casserole? I could...order something."

"You can carry something," Pru said, a smile ghosting in despite everything.

Deputy Barrett tipped her head toward her cruiser. "I'm heading back to the station. If anything feels off, you call me. If you think about going somewhere odd, you text me. If you even sneeze suspiciously, you let me know."

Freddie gave her a small salute. "Yes, ma'am."

"And Freddie?" Deputy Barrett added, softening. "I know I said this already, but it stands double now: I don't need heroes. I need you alive and unharmed."

Freddie's throat tightened. "Understood."

They split at the curb. Nigel loped away toward the theatre, patting his pockets for a non-existent cigarette to calm his nerves and then thinking better of the idea. Deputy Barrett slid behind the wheel and glanced up at them once more before pulling away. Pru took a to-go cup of hospital coffee out of Freddie's hand, tossing it in the nearby trash can, and made a face. "Let's get you something that doesn't taste like punishment."

Freddie managed a smile. "I should open the shop. It'll keep me from seeing that gauze square every time I blink."

"Then I'll put on a fresh pot and make sure Aggie doesn't unionize for more snacks," Pru said, looping her arm through Freddie's as they crossed the lot. "We'll tell people Father's alright. We'll accept casseroles on his behalf. We'll—what's the phrase—keep calm and carry on."

Freddie snorted. "Father Keating would approve."

They drove back into town with the windows cracked, the air thick and sweet with cut grass and hot pavement. When they passed St. Mary's, Freddie couldn't help but look: the bell tower rising, mute; the cottage next to it quiet as a held breath. She thought of Lynette's chair, of Winnie's chair, of the small unholy grace of a staged peace.

"Not natural causes," she murmured, the words hard as stones in her mouth. And then, because thinking like this could hollow a person out if she wasn't careful, she added, "We'll give Father Keating a proper cake when he's home. With too many candles."

Pru nodded fiercely. "And too much frosting." She said as she headed to the bakery for the afternoon.

Back at The Marple & Quill, the bell over the door chimed Freddie's return, the sound gentler than any hospital machine. The shop smelled like lemon oil and paper and the faintest scent of cinnamon. Aggie trotted out from behind a stack with the air of a manager demanding a status report.

"We're fine," Freddie told him, as if he'd asked. "And Father Keating will be, too."

Aggie blinked once, accepted this, and made for the small stripe of sunlight pooling across the front table.

Freddie unlocked the till, set the chalkboard sign to OPEN, and stood a moment with her palms on the counter, letting the familiar shape of the place steady her. People would come. They would ask how Father was. They would buy a paperback or a bookmark because it felt like doing something. She would sell them hope-bound stories and staple a receipt and say thank you, because routines were how you said to the world: I'm still here.

She tucked a fresh page into her small spiral notebook—the one Father Keating had told her to keep—and wrote, in tidy ink:

Hospital—Keating concussion.
Journal stolen.
Lynette staged (tea, book).
Winnie same.
Crowley watching. Change patterns.

She underlined the last one twice, closed the notebook, and slid it into her apron.

A MURDER MOST UNSOLVED

Then she flipped on the lamps, opened the blinds, and let the town back in.

***

Later that evening, Freddie was still shelving a new shipment of mysteries when the shop door rattled open. She frowned, it was past closing. Before she could protest, a cacophony of off-key kazoos and paper noisemakers filled The Marple & Quill.

"Happy birthday!" Pru shouted, her party hat askew but her grin enormous.

Behind her came Nigel, already flushed with excitement, Deputy Barrett with a rare mischievous spark in her eyes, and Kevin—dead serious as he carried an enormous cake like it was the crown jewels.

Freddie froze mid-step, clutching a hardback copy of *A Murder is Announced*. "What on earth..."

"Don't play coy," Pru scolded, sweeping forward to plant a kiss on Freddie's cheek. "You thought you'd sneak through your birthday unnoticed? Not in Fernridge, darling."

Kevin set the cake on the counter with reverence. "This took six hours. No one else was allowed near it. If Aggie so much as breathes on it—"

As if summoned, Aggie appeared on the counter in a swirl of fur and smugness. He sniffed the frosting, pawed delicately at the edge, and before anyone could intervene, sank his teeth into a frosted rosebud.

Kevin yelped. "He's desecrating it!"

Deputy Barrett burst out laughing, the sound loud and unguarded. "Guess he's claiming the biggest slice for himself."

Pru wagged a finger at the cat. "Greedy little beast. Save some for the humans."

Freddie's laughter came so suddenly that she clutched her stomach. She hadn't realized how badly she'd needed it.

They crowded into the reading nook, the cake lopsided but delicious once Kevin relented and sliced around Aggie's paw prints and teeth marks. Paper hats tilted, frosting smeared across napkins, and the shop filled with a warmth that hadn't touched Freddie in many years.

Deputy Barrett leaned back with her plate balanced on her knees. "So. Favorite birthday memory—go."

Nigel cleared his throat dramatically, as though about to recite Shakespeare. "Alas, I have none. My birthday was always overshadowed by Great-Aunt Lavinia's garden parties. Instead of cake, I got cucumber sandwiches. Instead of gifts, a pat on the head." He sighed heavily. "No one wants to celebrate a boy when a matriarch is holding court."

"Tragic," Pru said dryly. "Like the plot of a Victorian novel."

Kevin piped up. "Try being born on Christmas Eve. All my birthdays blurred into tinsel and hymns. My gifts were wrapped in red and green, and everyone claimed they were 'extra special' because it was two-in-one. They weren't. They were cheaper."

Deputy Barrett smirked. "My sixteenth was the best. Friends, a stretch limo, way too much perfume, and the feeling I could take over the world. We drove around for hours pretending we were famous."

Pru raised her glass of champagne. "Now that's a rite of passage."

"And yours?" Freddie asked softly.

Pru grinned like a cat with cream. "My thirty-something. Winnie and I went to Vegas. Painted the town red." She wagged her brows. "That's all I'll say."

Nigel gasped theatrically. "The mystery! The intrigue! Tell us more!"

"Never," Pru declared, tossing back the rest of her champagne.

They roared with laughter, Aggie batting at the dangling party streamers overhead. The little bookstore—usually hushed with the weight of old paper and these days quiet grief—buzzed with joy. For a moment, Freddie let herself forget the shadows gathering outside.

As the night wore on, they lingered over the crumbs of cake and empty glasses, trading more stories and inside jokes until their laughter blurred into the late hours.

It was Deputy Barrett who finally tilted her head and frowned. "Where's Aggie? I could use some kitty cuddles."

They searched every nook—the windowsill, the counter, the reading chair he often claimed as his throne. No cat.

Pru searched the kitchen, then froze. "Freddie," she called, her voice tight. "Come here."

The others hurried in. The back door stood open, the summer night pressing in heavy and dark. On the floor lay Aggie's collar, the little silver bell silent.

From outside came a frantic yowl.

They ran into the alley. There, tangled in a low tree branch, Aggie dangled upside down, eyes wild, tail thrashing. Beneath him, a note flapped in the night air, pinned cruelly to the bark.

Stop digging, or one of you is next.

Freddie's heart lurched. She freed Aggie, clutching him to her chest as his fur bristled.

The laughter of the evening vanished as if snuffed out by wind. Only the shadows remained, and the sick certainty that Crowley really was close and watching.

26

THE ORIGINAL LETTER

Morning light slanted through The Marple & Quill like folded ribbon, thin, bright, and a little forgiving. Pru had tucked a "GET WELL, FATHER KEATING" card beside the register for everyone who wished to sign and be delivered with a vase of zinnias pilfered from her own backyard. The bell over the door chimed now and then with ordinary customers and ordinary needs: a crossword-puzzle anthology, a paperback for the lake, a card that said *You're Doing Great, Sweetie* purchased by a man in his seventies.

Freddie breathed in the scent of paperbacks and decided, for the fifth time this hour, that if she kept her hands moving—straighten a display, refill the bookmark cup, wipe a nonexistent smudge from the counter—her brain might stop replaying the last two nights in looping, jittery bursts. Father Keating's bloody, bashed head, all that blood on his collar. Aggie hanging from a tree scared out of his wits.

Aggie now sprawled across the poetry section, an orange tabby apostrophe with a pulse. When Freddie passed, he thunked his head against her wrist and chirped for chin scratches. He seemed to have recovered quickly from his ordeal, for which Freddie was thankful.

The door chimed again. Nigel Ashcroft swept in like a man who'd forgotten he was famous and remembered again at the last second. His long vest trailed by a beat; and his oddly British brown hat. He wore that polished-lacquer posture of theater folk, but the varnish didn't quite cover the wear. Today, there was something raw around his eyes.

"Ah," he said, and his voice came out softer than his entrance warranted, "Miss March. Ms. Hawthorn. Aggie, you ungovernable prince."

Aggie flicked an ear. Pru looked up from retying a string on a bundle of recipe cards. "You look like you slept in your costume trunk," she said, kindly.

"I wrestled with a demon," Nigel replied, setting his folded hands on the counter like he was bracing for judgment.

"Run-of-the-mill?" Pru asked. "Or bespoke?"

"Shame," he said simply. "And its understudy, cowardice."

Freddie's stomach tightened. "What did you do?" It came out sharper than she meant.

Nigel flinched, then reached into the inside pocket of his coat with deliberate care. He set a thin, soft-edged bundle of paper on the counter. The folds had yellowed, the creases tattered with years. He didn't slide it toward her so much as lay it down with a hint of ceremony.

"I kept the letter," he said. "The one that became A Murder Most Unsolved. Not the envelope but the text itself. I made a photocopy the day it arrived, in case the original got lost in the production shuffle. I told myself it was purely practical. Then I told myself it was a shameful souvenir. Then I told myself to forget it existed. I did not forget. I used the photocopy for regular viewing, but I had the original in a safe."

Pru's brows shot up. "Nigel."

"I know." He looked at Freddie, and for once there wasn't a lick of performance in him. "I should have told you. I was afraid of what it might prove. I also had to have a friend back home mail it and until I was sure that was to happen, I didn't dare say a word. But after recent events…well, its importance has significantly increased as of late."

The bookstore noise went small around the edges. Somewhere outside, a truck downshifted with a sigh. Freddie made herself breathe and forgive Nigel, and his ego, for its attempted self-preservation. "Show me," she said with an edge of the impatience she felt for him.

Nigel unfolded the papers. It had the washed-out grayness of the ghosts of time; lines of type faded here and not there. He rotated it so it faced Freddie and stepped back as if he'd just placed a relic on its shrine.

She leaned in.

There was tea that night. A book left open, as if the words could keep watch. And a bell that forgot to keep time, struck wrong, wrong, wrong. None saw, but I did. I wrote it so I might not forget. The streets here remember, though they do not speak. The lone ruby eye at Elder & Main blinks but never saves. The river whispered, but he did not hear. He went down into the mouth of the stairs and his foot was not sure. I had not meant such a thing. I am telling you because I dare not tell them.

Freddie's scalp prickled. She felt herself reading slower, like the words were steps on a dark staircase.

"'The lone ruby eye at Elder & Main,'" she whispered. "That's our stoplight. The only one in town."

Pru's finger hovered over the line about the bell. "And 'forgot to keep time'—that summer the lightning strike fried the mechanism. They replaced the works before the festival."

Nigel's mouth twisted. "I told myself it could be any town, any stoplight, any bell. Actors are talented liars when the audience is themselves."

Freddie's eyes tracked the letter again. The cadence was odd—clipped and lyrical, as if the writer was trying to make a confession bearable by trimming it with flourish. There were more lines further down—brief, uncanny:

He carried patience in his pocket and did not deserve it. I took a little and then I took too much. The door was not locked. The tea was sweet.

She swallowed. The taste in her mouth was bitter, the bile of her hatred that grew for the letter writer.

Pru glanced at Nigel. "What did you change for the episode?"

"I sanded the names off," he said. "I made a vicar into a suspect and a widow into a witness. I... softened the edges. And then, because the truth would not let me, I left it unsolved."

Freddie smoothed the letter with her palm, careful not to smudge. A faintness was visible on the back—not print, not stain. Indentations. The paper had once been beneath another, and whoever wrote on top left pressure marks behind.

Her archivist brain clicked into gear like a well-oiled lock. "Hang on," she said. "Do you have a pencil?" She was already reaching for the cup by the register. "And something soft underneath—felt, a paper pad—yes."

Pru slid a folded length of tissue paper across. Nigel watched, rapt, as Freddie placed the letter face-down and began shading lightly along the backside with the side of the graphite, moving in gentle ovals. The trick wasn't to draw but to let the graphite catch the edges of absence.

Lines began to appear, ghostly at first, then resolving: curves, corners, a crisp, simple sequence. With how many years had passed since the letter was written, she couldn't believe it was actually working. Luck was indeed on her side today.

"Two... one..." Freddie breathed. "Four."

She shaded a little more, and the impression deepened: MOTOR COURT BOX 214—the faint block letters somewhat legible now.

Pru's whole face lit. "The Motor Court boxes," she said. "They used to rent them cash, no wonder we didn't find anything at the post office."

"Box two hundred fourteen," Nigel repeated softly, as if saying it made amends.

Aggie, sensing drama, relocated with the speed and self-importance of a star entering a scene. He planted himself squarely on the letter and thumped his tail over the penciled numbers like a censor bar.

"Good man," Pru said, kissing the top of his head. "Guard the evidence."

The bell above the door chimed a little musical triad, and two women entered in a waft of White Diamonds and powder. Ada and June—the town's unofficial busybodies—crossed the threshold like they were taking the stage.

"Mercy," Ada said, catching sight of Nigel, "it's *Father Grey* in our humble annex."

"I told you he shops for biscuits somewhere, Ada," June murmured. "This seems as good a place as any."

Pru put on her brightest bakery smile. "Ladies, what can we help you find? Nigel is for sale but quite a hefty price tag." Freddie winked and Nigel huffed.

"We're looking for cookbooks again," Ada said, setting her pocketbook on the counter like it might bolt. "My great nephew and his wife are finally here, and their diet has changed since last time. Apparently, they dine on 'microgreens' and 'foams' exclusively. I have never foamed anything but anger."

"Try *Simple Fancy*," Pru said, plucking a glossy spine from a stand. "Everything sounds like a restaurant and tastes like a potluck, though I'm not positive things are foamed."

June leaned an elbow on the counter, peering at the paper beneath Aggie. "What's that then?"

"A receipt," Freddie said smoothly, steering her toward the romance section with a conspiratorial crook of her finger. "And if you're still thinking of asking your neighbor out, *When Widows Woo* is back in stock."

June flushed a pleasant rose. "I wasn't—you don't—oh, give me that."

They drifted off. When they were out of earshot, Nigel exhaled. "Your town," he said, "is relentless."

"Isn't it wonderful?" Pru asked playfully.

Freddie slid the letter from under Aggie's satisfied weight and checked the impression again. BOX 214. There it was, inkless and undeniable. "Let's go see Penny," she said, already untying her smock. "If anyone on this planet can connect a box number to a human being with an unfortunate personality, it's her."

"Go," Pru said. "I'll mind the fort. I'm due for a good eavesdrop anyway."

"Bring back gossip," Ada called from the cookbook display.

"Bring back a husband," June added from the romance spinner.

Nigel, startled, patted his hair. "I'm only an actor," he stammered.

"We'll take what we can get," Ada said serenely.

The Fernridge Motor Court office smelled of burned coffee, mildew, and decades of accumulated paper. Penny Caldwell sat behind the laminate desk in a swivel chair that squeaked in Morse code. A fan wobbled in the corner, valiantly attempting to circulate the climate.

"You look like you're about to ask me to commit a minor crime," Penny said by way of greeting.

"Not a crime," Freddie said. "A recollection." She laid the shaded paper on the desk. "Do you remember who rented Box 214 back in '98? One of your boxes."

Penny's eyebrow climbed her forehead. "Well if that isn't a number from my nightmares." She opened a drawer and slid out a ledger so old it had developed personality. "Back then those boxes were cash-and-carry, no ID, may we never be that trusting again." She licked a finger, flipped. "Box two fourteen...here we are. 'E. Pike.' Two months prepaid. Notes say 'limp, cap, cash.'"

Nigel made a small noise, half regret, half vindication. "Pike," he echoed. "Our old friend."

Penny kept going. "Yup our old friend from room 6. Paid with crisp tens. No name on the receipt. Never wanted eye contact. Smelled like... machine oil." She squinted toward the ceiling. "The kind of man who leaves rooms as soon as he enters them."

Freddie's pen was already out; she wrote it down in her notebook.

Penny flipped the ledger shut with a satisfying slap. "You bringing me trouble, Winifred's girl?"

"Trying to carry some away," Freddie said.

Penny studied her face, then turned her attention to Nigel. "And you."

He straightened. "Yes?"

"Stay useful," she said. "Theatrical types can either gum the works or grease them. Your choice."

Nigel inclined his head as if she'd knighted him with a broom handle. "I shall be grease."

"Thank you," Freddie said, sincere down to the bones.

Penny waved a dismissive hand. "Don't thank me till you've poured bourbon on the grave of whatever nonsense this is." She pointed at the paper. "And keep that close. Paper's more honest than people."

Back at the shop, the zinnias looked brighter for the errand. Pru had sold *Simple Fancy* to Ada with a warning against foams and *When Widows Woo* to June with a wink and a coupon. Aggie had relocated to the front display like a benevolent gargoyle. On the chalkboard, Pru had scrawled: TODAY ONLY—BUY A COOKIE, GET UNSOLICITED ADVICE.

Freddie spread their treasures on the table in the back: Winnie's manila folder, the hollowed-out Christie, the sketch, the bracelet, the letter. The evidence made a kind of quiet constellation. She could almost draw lines between them with her finger.

Nigel hovered at the edge like a penitent altar boy. "Well?" he ventured.

"Well," Freddie said, "this proves the letter was written here. Here here. 'The lone ruby eye at Elder & Main' isn't poetry you pull from a map. It's lived-in words. It's Fernridge."

Nigel's shoulders sank with relief and something sadder. "Then I didn't invent a tragedy," he said. "I adapted one, like a thief in a library."

Pru nudged a mug toward him. "You didn't poison anyone," she said. "You didn't push anyone down a bell-tower. You didn't send threats or hit priests over the head. You wrote a story someone else handed you. That's not sin; that's art. Misguided, maybe. But you're in the clear."

Nigel blinked, looking both younger and older. "Do you mean that?"

She reached across and squeezed his hand, warm and firm. "I mean it. And now we need you on the right side of the footlights. You're staying until we finish this."

His answer came fast, like it had been waiting in him all day. "Yes."

Aggie, who had been washing a paw with excruciating elegance, chose that moment to stand, hop onto the table, and plant his considerable haunches atop the letter once more—as if a royal seal were required. Then he reached out a paw and, with surgical delicacy, hooked Freddie's pencil and dragged it a precise inch closer to him. *Mine now.*

"Fine," Freddie said, laughing despite the tight band around her ribs. "You can be head of forensics."

Freddie picked up her notebook and documented all the new details from the day's investigation.

Nigel watched the tidy lines of her handwriting like they were incantations. "Ink makes it seem real," he said.

"Ink makes it stay," Freddie replied.

Pru propped her chin on her fist. "What next?" she asked. "Besides telling Lila before she breaks in here and tells us for us."

"We tell Lila," Freddie said. "And we ask Father Keating, when he's stronger, whether his church records show Mrs. Lynette ever complained about a man hanging around the tower. But first..." She glanced at Nigel. "I think you should read the letter aloud. Once. Here. For her." She touched the folder—Winnie's handwriting, tea rings, red circles. "Then we put it away. And we move forward."

Nigel swallowed. "I don't know if I can do it without going full BBC," he murmured.

"Fine," Pru said. "Then do."

He stood, smoothed the paper, and began. His voice went richer by degrees, but he kept it tethered to the small room, to the old wood and the cat and the women who were listening because they loved someone who loved mysteries. The lines sounded different in his mouth—more human, less clue, like the confession of a man who'd tried to turn guilt into poetry so he could carry it.

By the end, Pru had two fingers pressed to her lips. Freddie had her notebook open on her knee, pencil between her teeth, not writing.

Outside, a truck rumbled past with a bed full of watermelons. Kids' laughter floated faintly from the sidewalk like wind chimes in a different key. Someone taped a flyer to the window for a community yard sale. Somewhere down the block, a single, stubborn cardinal practiced the same three notes over and over like it was studying for a test.

Nigel folded the letter. His hands were shaking.

"Thank you," Freddie said. She took the letter and slid it into a clear sleeve, then into an envelope, and finally into the hollowed-out

Christie with the tissue paper. Aggie gave an approving mrrow, as if to say: *archive secured*.

Pru wiped her eyes briskly with the heel of her palm and set about making tea with a kind of purposeful vengeance. "Toast?" she said. "To the moment when a ghost got a forwarding address."

"Only if we can toast to the living, too," Nigel said. "Winifred would insist I think."

Freddie poured, and they touched mugs, and for three breaths the world was just the four of them—their found little company, the hum of a town that stubbornly refused to stop being itself, the warmth of a priest's butter cookies in a tin somewhere down the block, a deputy's star sticker still affixed to a uniform sleeve.

Freddie's phone buzzed. A text from Deputy Barrett: *Report in if anything breaks. 4 p.m., my office, if you've got more. No heroics.* A second later: *How's Keating?*

Freddie typed back: *Headache. Stubborn. Himself. We found something. See you at 4. Promise re: heroics.* She added a cat emoji with a crown, and Deputy Barrett fired back a thumbs-up and then, inexplicably, a cake.

"Deputy Barrett, Lila, says no heroics," Freddie reported.

"Lila never says no pie," Pru countered, already slicing something that had not been there a moment ago.

Nigel moved to the window like a man who'd finally chosen his mark in a crowd—no more flitting, no more charm for sport. He tucked his hands into his pockets and watched Fernridge move through its afternoon. "I stayed in towns like this once," he said quietly. "When I was nineteen and needed to remember that work is not the only thing that makes a life worth having. I forgot that for a while."

"Remember it now," Pru said without looking up.

He smiled. "I'm trying."

Aggie leapt to his feet, trotted to the edge of the table, and batted the pencil back toward Freddie with the careful tap of a chess master making his move.

"All right," she told him, picking it up. "Here's ours." She drew another line on her page, an arrow connecting *Box 214* to *E. Pike* to *Silas Crowley*, then to *letter* then to *bell* then to *Daniel*. The arrowhead pointed toward a single word she wrote in block letters so firm it might as well have been carved:

ANSWER.

She underlined it once. Twice.

Then she looked up at her friends—her accomplices, her ridiculous, stubborn, good-hearted troupe—and felt the click of something in her chest that had nothing to do with clues and everything to do with courage.

"We're almost there," she said.

Pru slid a plate across. "Eat your courage with shortbread," she said. "It's more effective that way."

Nigel raised his mug. "To Winifred March," he said, voice steady at last. "Who kept a town stitched together with books, butter, and benevolence."

"To Winifred," Freddie and Pru echoed, the syllables soft and bright as the zinnias by the till.

Outside, the lone ruby eye at Elder & Main blinked its patient blink, keeping a quiet kind of time. Inside, Aggie sat down on the hollow book like a dragon on its hoard and closed his eyes. Which, if you asked anyone who loved him, counted as a vow.

A MURDER MOST UNSOLVED

They weren't done yet but they'd come a long way, and for now, Freddie wanted to celebrate and remember that.

27

A Furry Cannonball

The call came just after noon.

Penny's voice was tight as wire on the shop phone. "Freddie, you listening close?"

Freddie pressed the receiver tighter. "Yes. What is it?"

"Your mystery man calling himself E. Pike just came sniffing around again. Said he left something in Room Six. I didn't give him the key. Told him I'd have to check. He didn't argue—just stared too long and walked off toward Main Street but said he'd be back. Thought you'd want to know."

Freddie's pulse went quick and hard. She glanced toward Pru, who had been icing lemon cookies with enough force to qualify as exercise. "He's back," Freddie whispered.

Pru set down her piping bag. "Then so are we."

By the time they relayed it to Deputy Barrett, you could tell by the tone of her voice that she was set and ready. "Good. We'll catch him clean this time. You two do nothing except be my extra eyes since you've seen him before. Understood?"

"Understood," Freddie promised, though the knot in her stomach whispered that she'd already broken promises like that.

An hour later, the three of them were squeezed into the front window of the Fernridge Feed & Farm across from Penny's Motor Court. The bell over the door had a rusty jangle, and the place smelled like cracked corn, old rope, and the sweet molasses note of horse treats. A fan clattered lazily above sacks of seed, stirring dust into slow galaxies lofting through the air.

Pru had insisted they buy something so they didn't look suspicious; they now stood in front of a twine display, pretending to debate the merits of sisal versus jute while peeking through the cloudy front windows.

Deputy Barrett leaned casually against a rack of seed packets—marigold, bee balm, collards—her badge tucked but her presence unmistakable. She gave curt nods to the steady stream of locals who wandered in for dog food and garden gloves, but her eyes never left the Motor Court office across the street.

Mr. Clyde Harlan, still hawking raffle tickets for his wooden goose even off-duty, clomped past with a fifty-pound sack of scratch. "Afternoon, Deputy," he wheezed. "Storm's building up a mood."

"Afternoon, Mr. Harlan," Deputy Barrett said without moving her gaze.

At the counter, Bev—who knew every person in town by first and middle name—was ringing up Miss Tansy Ann Dell's bulk cat litter. Miss Tansy hummed a dramatic minor-key ballad to the bag as if it, too, needed encouragement.

"Tansy," Pru hissed under her breath, "don't you dare start singing 'I Will Survive' near the deputy."

"I would never," Tansy whispered, immediately clearing her throat for a high note.

Pru tapped a roll of twine against her palm. "You know, I think sisal says 'I tie things earnestly,' but jute says 'I tie things ironically.'"

Freddie would've laughed if her heart wasn't punching against her throat.

Deputy Barrett murmured without looking at them, "If he shows, I go. You stay. Do not try to be brave. Be smart."

"I can do both," Pru whispered. "But fine."

Freddie swallowed and turned back to the window. Outside, the world felt fat with weather. Clouds had gathered from the quarry end of town, darkening the edges of buildings; even the lone ruby eye—the stoplight at Elder & Main—looked thoughtful, pausing a beat longer between colors.

Then the door to Penny's office opened.

A man stepped out—tall, shoulders stooped, cap pulled low. Even at this distance, Freddie knew him. The uneven gait, the left foot dragging with a little outward turn. Silas Crowley.

He turned, and his gaze swept the street like a hawk's. For a strangled heartbeat, Freddie thought he would keep moving. Then his eyes landed square on her through the feed store window.

His whole body jolted.

"Uh-oh," Pru muttered.

"Stay put," Deputy Barrett hissed. But Crowley was already moving, fast. Faster than Freddie thought possible for someone with his limp. He cut across the street, through the feed store yard, shouldering past a pyramid of salt blocks that wobbled dangerously, and bolted down the back lane that sloped toward the quarry trail.

Deputy Barrett swore and changed her mind on what Freddie and Pru should do. "With me!" she shouted.

They burst out of the feed store. The bell clanged behind them; Miss Tansy's "Oh!" rose like a cymbal crash. Gravel skittered underfoot as they sprinted across the yard. A flock of startled sparrows burst from the eaves, the air suddenly wings and grit and the earthy tang just before rain.

Crowley was a jerking shadow ahead, weaving through broken fences and shrubs. He clipped a rusted hog feeder, bounced off a stack of pallets, and kept going. The storm clouds overhead cracked open with a low growl, wind lifting the smell of wet stone from the quarry ahead.

Freddie ran harder than she'd ever run, lungs burning, sneakers slipping on the packed dirt. Elder Lane fell away behind them. The weight of the past few weeks—the bell, the folder, the letters, the tea—hammered in time with her feet. Beside her, Pru kept pace with surprising speed for an aging pastry magician, muttering what sounded like bakery curses—"burnt crusts, collapsed soufflés"—under her breath.

"Left!" Deputy Barrett barked, reading the terrain three steps ahead. "He'll take the service path, less washout."

They cut down a little trail that smelled like crushed pennyroyal. Blackberry brambles snagged Freddie's jeans. A gust shouldered the trees; the first fat drops of rain struck the dust and lifted the petrichor that tasted like something old waking.

Crowley threw a glance over his shoulder, stumbled, then pushed on. The limp made his stride jerky, desperate, but adrenaline and a longing for his freedom propelled him. He aimed for the culvert that ran under the old quarry road, a low concrete oval dark and damp.

"Careful!" Pru gasped as the ground tilted slick. "Straighten your feet—no, Freddie, straighten your feet!"

"I don't know what that means!" Freddie wheezed, and then she did, instinctively, knees soft, weight forward, balance regained.

Then something bright orange streaked across the path ahead.

"Aggie?!" Freddie shrieked.

The cat, who should have been napping three blocks away on a stack of mystery paperbacks, shot out of the culvert like a furry cannonball, tail high, eyes blazing. He landed square in Crowley's path with a hiss so dramatic it belonged on a marquee.

"Where did he even—" Pru started.

"That cat!" Deputy Barrett said, somehow both breathless and composed.

Startled, Crowley faltered. His toe caught on a root. He went sprawling, palms scraping in the gravel with a sound that made Freddie's teeth ache. For a split second, he looked young with shock.

By the time he staggered upright, Deputy Barrett had closed the gap, gun drawn but steady, stance low and unequivocal.

"Silas Crowley!" she barked. "Don't move. Hands where I can see them."

He froze, chest heaving, eyes ricocheting between the deputy, Freddie, and the furious orange cat holding court at his feet like a magistrate.

"Don't!" Deputy Barrett warned as his right heel twitched.

Crowley lifted his hands, fingers splayed. Rain beaded on the brim of his cap and ran off in thick lines. Thunder rolled somewhere nearer, as though the sky had decided to lean in.

A confession broke out of him in ragged bursts, like a dam giving way.

"I didn't mean it," he stammered. His voice had that caged-bird flutter, a stutter that caught on consonants and turned them to wire. "I—I was stealing—just coins, just the donation box up by the b-bell. People leave their quiet money there. I lost my j-job after the injury. I was hungry. I was—" He swallowed so hard it looked like it hurt. "He—he surprised me. D-Daniel. He wasn't supposed to be there."

Freddie's chest hollowed. Her dad's name ripped the air, hitting her square in the heart.

Crowley's words tumbled faster, desperate, as if saying them could rewind time. "He grabbed my arm, shouted—I p-panicked. We struggled. He slipped. Or I p-pushed. I don't know anymore. But I lost the donation box key in the struggle, n-o money a-anyway." His breath came in sawtooth pulls. "He fell. The crawlspace—the one behind the ladder, where the old boards cover the p-pulley anchors—there's a space. I shoved him there. I thought no one would ever—" His face cracked. "I thought no one would ever find him."

Freddie felt the ground tilt. There it was—the rot beneath the town's pretty paint. She had dreamed this moment and dreaded it, had asked for truth and now had to swallow it like glass.

"And, that lady, L-Lynette—" Crowley's eyes went wide and unfocused, the past rising like floodwater. "She saw him fall. From her cottage window. She c-came storming across the yard next morning, said she'd tell the p-priest, tell the p-police, tell the whole world. I—I gave her tea. Foxglove. Said it was herbs for her nerves while I "explained" what happened, told her she mis-saw. She drank it." He shuddered. "She... she went quiet. Just like the TV show. Just like I wrote."

Nigel's script—*A Murder Most Unsolved*—echoed between Freddie's ears. The staging. The tea. The book.

"You wrote the letter," Freddie whispered. It came out like a verdict and a prayer.

His head jerked in a miserable nod. "It was eating me alive. I couldn't tell anyone here. So I wrote it down, sent it away. A story I could live with. The actor—your man—he made it b-beautiful. A riddle instead of a sin."

Freddie's stomach rolled. "And Winnie?" Her voice was not a question. It was a blade she had to pick up.

He flinched. "Winnie... recognized me. At first I thought—she's old, what does she know? But she looked at me like a person looks when the last piece of the puzzle clicks." His mouth trembled. "She knew. She knew. I saw it in her eyes. She'd tell. I couldn't— I couldn't let that happen. Not after all these years being careful. I took foxglove from the parsonage beds. Crushed just enough to taste like bitterness you could explain. She sipped it like the other. Sat in her chair with her book, like sleep."

Pru made a sound that was part sob, part curse. Freddie's hands had gone numb; she realized she was gripping Pru's sleeve, pressing crescents into her friend's skin.

Crowley sagged as if the telling had extracted whatever scaffolding kept him upright.

Deputy Barrett's voice was iron. "Don't move."

He let out a small, breaking laugh. "Where would I go?" He glanced toward the quarry, then up at the bell tower that peeked above the tree line, white steeple smudged gray by weather. "He never left," he said, almost wonderingly. "Not really."

Thunder cracked directly overhead, so loud the ground jumped. Somewhere down-mountain, the quarry face returned it—a dull, weary boom.

Deputy Barrett stepped in, smooth and practiced. "Turn around. Interlace your fingers."

He obeyed, trembling. The metallic click of cuffs snapped the air like punctuation.

"You have the right to remain silent," Deputy Barrett recited, clear and steady, the cadence of a woman who meant every word she said. "Anything you say can and will be used against you in a court of law. You have the right to an attorney..."

Her words echoed against the quarry walls, final and inescapable. Crowley closed his eyes as she spoke, rain slicking his lashes into spikes. Aggie sat, tail wrapped around his paws, like a small, indignant judge.

Deputy Barrett called it in, voice clipped. "One in custody. Send a unit and call St. Mary's—we'll need a scene team for the tower crawlspace." She paused, listening, then added, "And get Penny Caldwell a statement form, she's our first alert."

Penny's old truck idled up at the road above, her face pale but resolute behind the windshield. When she saw the cuffs flash, she sagged forward against the wheel for a second, then straightened, mouth set. Bev from the feed store had hustled out with a broom like she might sweep up the crime, and Clyde hovered uncertainly, wooden goose raffle book still tucked under his arm.

Freddie stood rooted, heart hammering so hard she could barely hear Pru's voice. Her hearing tunneled weirdly: the hiss of rain on gravel, the faint tin-tin-tin of a loose sign, Aggie's sharp little sneeze as a drop hit his nose. She could see everything and nothing. Her father's name had hung in rooms without walls for years. Now it was here, heavy and real.

"Freddie," Pru said, gripping her shoulders. "He said it. He admitted it all. Daniel. Lynette. Winnie. It's over."

"Not over," Freddie said automatically, hoarse. "But... different." The word felt right. She wasn't at the edge of a cliff anymore; she was on a path—muddy, treacherous, but a path—with names nailed to posts.

At her feet, Aggie shook raindrops from his whiskers and gave a satisfied mrrow, as if to say: You're welcome. He butted his head against Freddie's shin with a force that nearly toppled her.

She bent and scooped him up, soaking wet fur plastering to her skin, the weight of him anchoring her as everything else slid. "You just earned a lifetime of treats, you ridiculous hero," she whispered into his fur. Aggie rumbled like a small engine.

Pru exhaled a shaky laugh. "Better order a whole pallet."

Deputy Barrett guided Crowley up the trail, steady but not cruel, a firm hand on his elbow. As they reached the road, a second cruiser pulled in, lights splashing red and blue across the wet. Miss Tansy, who had followed at a distance holding her cat litter like an infant, began to hum a minor-key Kyrie Eleison that was fitting.

Nigel appeared at a jog, jacket dark with rain, breath fogging. He took in the scene—the cuffs, the deputy, the cat—and went very still. "Is it—?"

"It's him," Pru said, wiping at her face with the heel of her hand, laugh-crying. "It's finally him."

Nigel's gaze found Freddie. For once, he did not perform. He only bowed his head, rain stippling his hair flat. "I'll give a statement," he said roughly, "to whatever you need about the letter. How it came. How it sounded. How a story can be a knife if you let it."

Deputy Barrett lifted her chin. "I'll take it. Later." Her eyes softened, just a shade, as they settled on Freddie. "We'll get a team up there." She looked toward the steeple, storm-shadowed and tall. "We'll bring him home."

The words hit Freddie with the force of a bell strike. Bring him home. The phrase got under her ribs and pushed until her lungs remembered how to breathe. She nodded. "Thank you," she managed, and meant not just for the promise, but for the steadiness.

They began to move, Deputy Barrett and her officers to coordinate, Nigel to confer with Penny and Bev, Pru to herd Freddie toward a bit of overhang where the rain fell less like needles and more like a blessing. Clyde pressed an umbrella into Freddie's hand with solemnity that would've suited a coronation. "This one's lucky," he declared. "Never flips inside out, not even in a mood."

"Thank you, Mr. Harlan," Freddie said, voice wobbling into a little laugh despite everything.

Kevin arrived at a pant, drenched, holding a cardboard carrier like a newborn. "I brought coffee," he announced, as if he had just invented it. "Hot. Strong. Emergency strength."

"You're a saint," Pru said, grabbing a cup and shoving it into Freddie's hands.

Freddie wrapped her fingers around the heat, the steam fogging her eyes. Around them, the town did what good towns do: it adjusted itself to cradle a hard thing. People spoke in low voices, offered napkins, turned away at the right moments, and turned toward those who needed them.

Deputy Barrett returned, a sleeve dark with rain, a strand of hair untidily plastered to her temple, human again under the uniform. "Crew is heading to the tower. We'll tape off the base and do this right." She paused. "You don't have to be there, Freddie."

"I know," Freddie said. "But I want to be somewhere I can see the steeple."

Deputy Barrett's mouth twitched. "You sound like Keating." Then, quieter: "He'll be glad when he hears."

"He will," Freddie said, feeling the warm rush of that, too. She pictured Father Keating's steady hands, his butter cookies, the way he'd said, *You belong as you show up.* She would show up.

Rain slackened and then steadied, the storm deciding on its mood. The bell—newly fixed years ago, then the subject of so much whispered history—was silent. It wouldn't toll until there was something to toll for.

They waited. Not long—twenty minutes, maybe thirty—but long enough for the adrenaline to slide into bone-deep shaking. Pru tucked Freddie under her arm like a wing. Nigel hovered, uncharacteristically quiet, an umbrella forgotten at his side, rain spangling his sleeve. Aggie shifted in Freddie's grip and then leapt down with a wet *splat*, marching in indignant figure eights between their ankles as if to herd them all into calmness.

Up the hill, yellow tape appeared. Figures moved at the base of the tower—slow, deliberate. A word came down, relayed from mouth to mouth along the narrow path, changing only in volume, not in meaning.

"Found."

Freddie did not hear the word; she felt it. It passed through the crowd like a warm wind and landed in her chest. Pru's breath hitched. Nigel's eyes went wet. Penny put a fist to her mouth. Mr. Harlan removed his cap.

Deputy Barrett touched Freddie's elbow and looked at her—not with pity, but with the kind of recognition you give someone when they have reached a shore. "We'll do this with care," she said. "I promise you."

Freddie nodded. She couldn't make her throat work yet, but she nodded. The rain softened further, each drop precise and singular, as if the sky had remembered itself and was embarrassed for the scene it had made.

They didn't see more than that; the rest belonged to professionals and to reverence. But the steeple stood against the clearing storm, and the town stood with it, and Freddie—who had come back to Fernridge to answer a letter and found herself holding history by its ragged corner—let herself lean for a moment into Pru's shoulder and breathe.

Aggie butted her calf again, and when she looked down, he blinked up at her with the yellow-eyed gravity of the profoundly sure. If a cat could say *See?*, he did. If a cat could say *Stay*, he did that, too.

"Okay," Freddie whispered to him, to the steeple, to the woman she used to be and the one she was right now. "Okay."

Deputy Barrett finished with Crowley and closed the cruiser door. The lights painted the wet road into a ribbon of unlikely color. Nigel finally opened his umbrella. Pru, of course, refused, holding her face to the rain like a dare.

"Back to the shop?" Pru asked.

"In a minute," Freddie said, eyes on the tower. "Just... let me watch the bell."

They stood until the thunder was only a memory and the rain was a whisper. The town breathed with them. Somewhere, a child laughed at a puddle. Somewhere else, Miss Tansy tried—and failed—to remember the second verse of a hymn and made one up that was better.

And at Freddie's feet, Aggie sat like a furry little squire guarding a queen, tail curled, chin high, receiving the praise that would follow. She bent and scratched his chin. "Key to the city, sir," she murmured. "Shaped like a sardine."

He closed his eyes, gracious in his victory.

As Deputy Barrett's cruiser eased away with its grim cargo and the scene crew settled in for careful, necessary work, Freddie felt it settle in her bones, too—not fear. Not the scorched edge of grief. Resolution, yes. But also something else, small and surprisingly gentle.

Home.

28

THE QUIET AFTER

The days following Silas Crowley's arrest unspooled like a town holding its breath. Fernridge—so often noisy with gossip, porch music, the hum of lawnmowers—moved quieter now, the way a body does after an injury, waiting to see if it has healed or just stopped bleeding. Fernridge and Freddie were changed, all for the better.

The bell tower was taped off, crews came and went with clipboards, and the Gazette ran two extra editions with headlines so stark they looked borrowed from a larger city. But in the hush that followed, it wasn't headlines Freddie carried with her. It was the image of Crowley's hunched shoulders, the sound of her father's name said aloud like truth at last, and the sight of Aggie crouched in the rain, daring the past to move one inch further.

They all went to the hospital to visit Father Keating. His concussion had faded into a bruised line on his temple, and his sense of humor had reasserted itself with vigor.

"I am deeply ashamed," he told them as they clustered around him. "Imagine—missing the most dramatic chase Fernridge has seen since Clyde Harlan tried to drive his lawnmower to Knoxville."

"Father," Freddie said, exasperated but smiling despite herself, "you were hit on the head."

"Yes, but in fairness, so was St. Peter of Verona, and he still managed to write letters. I only managed a nap and eat some very poor soup." He waved at the tray with disdain. "Chicken noodle, without conviction."

Deputy Barrett stood near the door, arms crossed. "You nearly cracked your skull. You've nothing to be ashamed of."

Father Keating tipped his head, eyes twinkling. "Then I shall instead be ashamed of my hospital gown. It was a horror. Don't let anyone bury me in that thing."

Even Pru laughed, which was saying something; she had been brittle since the chase, her jokes sharp around the edges. Nigel, on the other hand, had become oddly tender, filling for Father Keating he produced a tin of shortbread from his coat like a magician pulling a dove from a sleeve.

"For when they finally free you," he said solemnly. "Hospital food is a crime in itself."

Father Keating accepted it as a sacrament. "Bless you, Mr. Ashcroft. The Lord moves in mysterious tins."

Freddie, watching it all, felt her breath ease for the first time since the storm.

Later that night, they gathered at Pru's bakery kitchen, still warm from ovens gone idle, to take stock. Pru leaned against the counter, arms folded, her hair haloed by flour dust. Nigel perched nearby, far too close, picking stray icing off the counter with one finger.

"You're a menace," she told him flatly.

"A charming menace," he said, flashing his best *Father Grey* grin.

"Charming like a raccoon in the pantry," she replied, though she didn't step back when he leaned closer.

Kevin, slicing lemon bars in the background, muttered, "God help us all."

Freddie half-listened, half-dreamed. For all her skepticism, it looked like Nigel might just stay longer than his usual disappearing act. And maybe, she thought with a wry smile, Fernridge was odd enough to make room for him.

The true healing began at The Marple & Quill. One Thursday evening, Freddie flipped the sign to CLOSED but left the lamps burning and the curtains open. Chairs were pulled in a circle, mismatched and creaky, just as Winnie had always liked it.

Deputy Barrett arrived straight from duty, uniform still neat, but she brought pie from the diner and deposited it on the counter with an awkward shrug. Kevin carried a tray of tiny cucumber sandwiches, explaining solemnly that "mystery-solving required finger food." Nigel wore a scarf far too dramatic for a small-town reading circle, but nobody complained.

Pru set out teacups. "We're calling this circle Winnie's Girls," she announced.

Nigel sniffed. "Even though I am manifestly not—"

"You are when I say you are," Pru cut in.

Kevin raised a sandwich. "Hear, hear."

Freddie laughed, the sound startling in its freedom. She reached behind the counter and hung the glitter-crusted paper crown—the same one from her childhood, edges dulled but still valiant—on the hook beside the register.

"She would've wanted us to read tonight," Freddie said. "Not mourn. Not gossip. Just... read."

"What's first?" Deputy Barrett asked.

Freddie lifted a well-loved copy from the stack. "*Murder at the Vicarage.*"

A delighted noise came from the doorway. Father Keating, still pale but stubbornly upright, leaned in on his cane. "Well now," he said. "If you're going to start with the Vicarage, I refuse to sit this one out."

They made space for him without a word. He sat, Aggie immediately curling into his lap as if to stamp approval.

And together, under the amber glow of the bookstore lamps, they began. Words wove out across the circle, the sound of pages and voices binding them tighter than any secret could.

The night wore long, voices blurring with tea and pie, laughter spilling soft against the windowpanes. Stories overlapped, grief softened at the corners, and for the first time since Winnie's death, Freddie felt Fernridge breathe like a single body. Wounded, mending, but whole.

When the others had gone, she stayed to tidy, stacking cups, brushing crumbs into her palm. Aggie padded after her like a shadow. She paused at the register, fingers brushing the crown, the glitter still clinging after all these years.

29

HOME.

Weeks later, she unlocked the door of The Marple & Quill. Morning air rushed in, cool and damp with dew. Aggie hopped into the front window, tail flicking once before curling into the sunbeam that would soon arrive.

Freddie flipped the sign to OPEN.

"Long may we read," she whispered.

And Fernridge, beyond the glass, seemed to nod in reply.

A postcard slid through the mail slot. The front showed a grainy photo of Nigel Ashcroft in his *Father Grey* cassock, standing on the steps of some old stone theatre, his hand raised in benediction.

On the back, his scrawl filled the space, barely contained by the printed lines:

"*My dearest Freddie, The Father Grey Anniversary Tour is tolerable, if lacking Fernridge's lemon bars. I must confess, however, that Fernridge remains my favorite stage. And I'll be back before you know it. — Yours, N.A.*"

Freddie smiled, shaking her head. Leave it to Nigel to treat the whole town like his personal encore.

Down the street, Pru's bakery window boasted new painted letters: **CHERRY VICTORY SWIRLIES — LIMITED RUN!**

A cluster of kids were already pressing noses to the glass, their breath fogging the pane. Pru had promised the flavor was "inspired by triumph" and sprinkled with edible glitter. Freddie suspected it was really inspired by Pru's delight in naming things dramatically, but that was fine too.

Back at the bookstore, the bell over the door jingled and a small girl emerged clutching a brand-new copy of *The Secret of the Old Clock*. The book was almost too big for her hands, but she hugged it like treasure. Freddie watched her skip down the steps and heard Winnie's voice clear as anything:

Spells wear off. Stories don't.

The words fluttered through Freddie's chest, landing gently.

***

Later that afternoon, cardboard boxes arrived from the city. They were stamped with shipping labels and scuffed from travel, but inside were the small pieces of Freddie's old life—books, trinkets, sweaters that smelled faintly of the apartment radiator, a teapot she rarely used. Though her time in Fernridge had taught her that she appreciated tea almost more than her Diet Coke habit, so there might be more teapots in her future.

She carried them upstairs, one by one, to the little apartment over the shop. Her books slid easily onto Winnie's old shelves, her kettle looked perfectly at home on Winnie's stove, her patchwork quilt brightened Winnie's bed. Instead of clashing, their lives meshed, like two chapters bound into one story.

Halfway through hauling the boxes, a voice called from the doorway:

"Need a hand?"

Lila—no badge, no stiff deputy title today, just *Lila*—stood with her sleeves rolled up. Without waiting for an answer, she grabbed the heaviest box and started up the stairs. "You should've told me this was happening today," she said over her shoulder.

"I didn't want to trouble you," Freddie replied.

Lila snorted. "You've already survived poisoned tea, falling sandbags, and foot pursuits. The least I can do is help you survive moving boxes."

They laughed together, the sound echoing up the narrow stairwell.

"Silas Crowley has confessed to everything," Lila eventually told Freddie. Her voice was warmer than the crisp deputy tone she usually used, a touch of kindness in every word. "He's been almost eager to unburden himself with the whole truth. I think it was eating him alive."

"I'm glad he's finally confessing and that he'll be held accountable," Freddie said, the words catching but true.

Lila nodded. "We recovered Father Keating's journal and the missing church bulletins. He tried to burn them in a dumpster behind the Motor Court. They're too charred to be much use, but with his confession, we don't really need them anymore."

Freddie swallowed hard and simply nodded.

"There's one more thing you should know," Lila went on, her gaze steady. She hesitated, as though measuring whether Freddie wanted the rest. "It's about Winnie."

Freddie's breath caught, but she gave the smallest nod for her to proceed.

"He admitted he knew she recognized him. He wasn't sure how much she'd pieced together, but he couldn't risk her unraveling it all—especially his connection to your father and Lynette." Lila's voice thinned. "He said he broke into her kitchen while she was busy in the shop and swapped some of her teabags with ones laced with foxglove. Then he waited, watching through the front glass." She paused, her jaw tight. "He said it was peaceful. She just... drifted. When he thought it was over, he came inside and tried to take back the tea cup and poisoned bags. That's when Aggie attacked him. That's what caused the broken cups and scattered books."

Freddie's tears blurred everything into watercolor. "Thank you," she whispered, voice thick. "I'm glad it was peaceful, to know that she wasn't in pain."

Lila reached across the counter and took Freddie's hand, giving it a firm squeeze. "Me too," she said softly.

Aggie meowed, pulling them back to the task at hand. He then supervised the whole moving-in affair with the dignity of a foreman. He leapt from one box to another, tail twitching, sniffing each as if inspecting the contents. Finally, he curled into a half-empty box of sweaters and biscuits tins, turned once, and plopped down with a decisive *thud*.

"Looks like he's found his spot," Lila said, amused.

"His Goldilocks box," Freddie agreed. "Just right."

Aggie blinked solemnly, as if declaring ownership.

Freddie looked around the room. At the blend of her things and Winnie's things, at the shelves, the stove, the window spilling light across the quilt—and felt something steady take root.

This wasn't temporary. This was home.

30

LONG MAY WE READ

The light in The Marple & Quill had shifted to a golden, late-morning sun pooling through the front windows and stretching across the rug in long, drowsy stripes. She should have been unpacking, but for now, she sat cross-legged on the floor, a half-written letter on her lap and a steaming cup of tea at her side.

Freddie tapped her pen against her chin, glanced down at the letter again, and then smiled as inspiration finally hit her.

Dear Nigel,

Thank you for the postcard. Your signature was almost as dramatic as your stage exits. I'm glad Father Grey's anniversary tour is giving you standing ovations, but I'll selfishly admit Fernridge feels a little quieter without you quoting Shakespeare while juggling scones.

The shop is settling around me in the nicest way. I'm not just house-sitting anymore. I'm home-sitting.

You were right about Winnie. She always knew more than she let on. But what I didn't know was how much she had shaped me. Or how ready I was to grow into someone who could run a place like this.

Come back soon. Our reading circle is eagerly awaiting your return.

With gratitude,
Freddie

She set the pen down and folded the letter with care. As she reached for an envelope, her gaze wandered toward the shelves, now filled with her own books nestled beside Winnie's.

Boxes were slowly disappearing – very slowly, their contents finding homes on shelves and in drawers. Their mugs shared the same hook. Their quilts layered across the back of the sofa like old and new stories folded together. Freddie had rearranged the front table display twice, experimented with cinnamon-scented candles over lemon polish, and even figured out the trick to the old stove's pilot light just in time for autumn weather to start sneaking up.

Aggie, ever the dignified resident, now claimed the sunniest chair by the window as his domain. Occasionally, he allowed visitors a gentle paw-tap of acknowledgment but only if they brought treats.

The bell over the door jingled, and Lila stepped inside holding a steaming cup and a pastry box. "Brought reinforcements," she said, waving the cup like a flag.

Freddie looked up from the books. "If that's Pru's scone, you're officially my favorite person this week."

"Pru made the raspberry almond ones today. I had to elbow an old woman with a cane to get this," Lila smirked, setting the box down proudly.

They shared a laugh, the kind that echoed softly through the shelves.

Lila's gaze wandered around the shop, lingering on the freshly painted sign near the register—*The Marple & Quill, Curated by Winifred & Winifred March*. "You've made it feel like her," she said.

Freddie nodded. "It's starting to feel like me too."

And it was. A blend of past and present, grief and growth, stacked on every shelf and folded into every cozy corner.

Freddie crossed to the door, flipped the sign to *OPEN*, and whispered with quiet certainty, **"Long may we read."**

About the Author

Sarah Dosher is a New York Times and USA Today Bestselling Author, born and raised in rural Oklahoma, where she still resides with her teenage twins, who keep life delightfully unpredictable. By day, she navigates the demanding world of healthcare and higher education, and by night, she pours her passion into the keyboard, weaving stories filled with intrigue and heart.

Though it's been nearly a decade since her last publication, she has never stopped writing, and she's eager to return to the publishing world with renewed passion. A lifelong book addict and devoted fan of British murder mysteries, Sarah's love of reading first sparked her journey as an author, and that passion continues to fuel her stories today.

Find her at sarahdosher.com.

www.ingramcontent.com/pod-product-compliance
Lightning Source LLC
Chambersburg PA
CBHW031147020426
42333CB00013B/545